I0087039

PASSION, PURPOSE, PLAN

How to Spot and Seize True Success

STEVEN D. COMPTON

PASSION, PURPOSE, PLAN by Steven D. Compton

© 2017 Steven D. Compton. All rights reserved.

No part of this book may be reproduced in any written, electronic, recording, or photocopying without written permission of the publisher or author. The exception would be in the case of brief quotations embodied in the critical articles or reviews and pages where permission is specifically granted by the publisher or author.

Although every precaution has been taken to verify the accuracy of the information contained herein, the author and publisher assume no responsibility for any errors or omissions. No liability is assumed for damages that may result from the use of information contained within.

Books may be purchased by contacting the publisher and author Steven D. Compton at:

Address: 5050 Union Street Box#325, Union City, GA 30291
Website: www.stevendcompton.com
E-mail: stevendcompton@gmail.com

ISBN: 0998801003
ISBN 13: 9780998801001

1. Business 2. Insurance 3. Faith 4. Inspiration

First Edition
Printed in United States of America

TABLE OF CONTENTS

1

MISTAKE BY THE LAKE

If I was going to be successful, I knew I had to be different.
The odds were stacked against me everywhere else.

~Steven D. Compton

I grew up hearing that Cleveland had a dark cloud over it, and it still does for many. I admit, my time in Cleveland was depressing at times. The truth is, people work hard in Cleveland. And they work a lot, which doesn't leave much time for leisure. Like most of us born and raised in Cleveland, I'm constantly reminded of Cleveland's unpopularity with the rest of the world. According to an unofficial source, Cleveland does have more cloudy days than sunny ones. It is one of the ten cloudiest cities in America.

I believe this idea that Cleveland is depressing stems from the hard-working personas of steelworkers dating back to the Industrial Revolution and lasting all the way up to the late 1900s. Steelworkers, union men, and factory workers aren't exactly cuddly types. They're more the salt of the earth. You take them seriously. They're more five o'clock shadows, hard hats, grit, and dirt than unicorns and rainbows. Public relations firms are probably very challenged to find something fun to promote about our town.

Even the entertainment in Cleveland is plagued with negative connotations. Sports teams like the Browns, Indians, and Cavaliers have been the laughingstocks of professional sports for more than fifty years. But it's not just sports. The motion picture industry took jabs and poked fun of my beloved city with movies like *Major League*, *Howard the Duck*, *Beverly Hills Cop*, and countless more.

Let me state the obvious. I'm originally from Cleveland, Ohio, the "Mistake by the Lake." Chicago is the "Windy City," New York City is the "Big Apple," and as long as we're talking catchy marketing slogans, they called my hometown the "Plum." This was a marketing ploy made in the eighties by city and state officials to attract people to the little big city. It didn't catch on.

I wanted to paint a picture for you, not of inspiration, but of desperation. The same picture of negative imagery that thousands of young people, including myself, have been afflicted by while growing up in blue-collar towns isn't limited to Cleveland. It's a problem all over the country, from Skid Row in LA to Detroit, or any town, large or small, that has the same reputation and challenges I've described. It's hard to tell children they can be anything they want to be or they can change the world when nothing good has come from where they live. Negative imagery can be detrimental to children's psyches. This also goes for parents and other adults around them.

Everybody in my family worked hard. Either they were in the education field, or they worked in factories or for the steel industry. I knew that I didn't want to work that hard for the rest of my life. I knew that if I was going to be successful, I had to do something different. The odds were stacked against me. There weren't many relatable images of success in my life at that time. I didn't have people around who encouraged me to be different or have high hopes for the future, so I spent most of my adolescence trying to find my way to success.

At the same time the steel industry was dying in the Great Lakes, a new occupational path was presented to the youth in Cleveland and other inner cities. That path was drug trafficking. When thousands of Vietnam vets returned home in the 1970s, they came back with the habits they had developed to cope with the war, so it wasn't long before drugs infested Cleveland.

In the late 1980s, the crack/cocaine epidemic practically destroyed our communities. But this problem also created a new economy, one that gave financial opportunity to millions of young men who were willing to risk their lives and freedom in hopes of seizing the deceiving rewards that drug trafficking offered. For decades strong, this demented system of false success created thousands of millionaires while destroying countless more lives.

Birthed by a need to survive financially and fueled by the false imagery of "hood success," millions of young men were introduced to entrepreneurship, only not in a way that they would ever legally succeed. Drug traffickers operated on the same premise as any other small business: supply and demand, inventory, distribution, suppliers, bookkeeping, ROI, profit and loss, employees, competitors, and marketing. Despite numerous legal and illegal threats against the drug business, drug traffickers had a powerful and compelling image of success in the hood. They dressed well and had a lot of cash to flash.

In fact, most of the more successful dealers had more money than they knew how to handle. Their excess money led to excess lifestyles: luxury cars, expensive clothes, and jewelry. Rap videos and gangster movies portrayed this lifestyle as acceptable, desirable, and easy to come by, if you were willing to take the risk. But the risks themselves were lies. No one talked much about the downside of dealing.

I saw it; I couldn't help but see it. It was all around me. You didn't have to choose to sell drugs; you had to choose not to, and that wasn't a popular choice to make. So, like millions of other young men during this time, I went along with the flow.

The drug game became an inherent part of me, and it would remain a part of me for a very long time. It wasn't until I found the meaning of true success that I was able to make better choices. Those choices included staying away from drugs, not chasing the almighty dollar, and more importantly, building a relationship with God. That's right. Drugs aren't the only false success in this world, and drug dealers aren't the only ones influenced by images of false success. False success is the belief that you will obtain success by pursuing riches, fame, and material things without putting in hard work, time, and pursuing your true passion.

Most law-abiding, God-fearing, all-American, and hardworking people are chasing the same empty dream as drug dealers. The one they're chasing is just as intoxicating as the life of a dealer. And just like the typical ending of a dealer's life, that pursuit will lead you to disappointment, unfulfillment, and possibly death. Maybe not physical death, but definitely a death of the dream.

I've been there. I've chased that drug dealer's dream and others like it, so I'm speaking from firsthand experience. This is the reason why I chose to write this book. I wanted to expose the ideology of false success, and I wanted to teach people two things: the true meaning of success, and how to find your path of true success and leave the empty paths behind.

As false and foundationless as drug dealing was, it presented a strong image of success to me and others around me. I know now that it was a false success, but during my adolescence, it was a powerful image of real success. How could it not be? It was an image of money, power, control, and freedom. It was illegal and had to be hidden, but it was the most powerful role model and image of business I had at the time. It's a funny thing about images. They shape your thoughts about yourself and how you view who and what you are. How you see yourself determines the level of self-esteem you have. And that level of self-esteem dictates how far you will go in life—how successful you can or will be. No matter how talented, smart, good, capable, or competent you are, if you don't see yourself as all those things, you'll never get anywhere. It's like having a full tank of gas and no gas pedal. The fuel is there, but you can't access it.

The really odd thing is, if you don't have talent, skill, or smarts, but you have high self-esteem based on false success, you'll go very far! Unfortunately, that false success held in high esteem will lead you away from the "true plan" for your life. Reality will catch up with you and crush your progress. Ultimately, you'll end up in pain, disappointment, and maybe even death.

I may or may not be the first one to tell you this, but there is another way. If you're reading this, you're already curious. Keep reading. You may be torn between giving up what you know, what you think is working, and what appears to be true success. But something inside you is eating at you, telling you there's something better. Listen to that voice. It knows something you're not aware of yet. It can lead you to your destiny. If you ignore it, you can take yourself off the path.

2

ENTREPRENEURSHIP

A business idea that doesn't go as planned is not a failure—
it's just a very painful and expensive lesson.

~Steven D. Compton

I knew I had to be different to be successful in life. Being different meant not following what most of my friends were doing in the hood. Now, I know it wasn't the false success of drug dealers that intrigued me. It was their ability to make money on their terms: when they wanted to, how they wanted to, and how much they wanted to. This was entrepreneurship at its roots. I didn't know at the time that this interest in life would lead me to a career in insurance and financial services. Most people do not know or understand what entrepreneurship takes. So, let me give you aspiring entrepreneurs the true definition of entrepreneurship:

> *"Entrepreneurship is the ability to make money on your terms; when*
> *you want to, how you want to, and how much you want to."*

Part of the "big lie" about finding the plan for your life is that some-how you'll just know what it is you want to do before you even do it. For instance, some kids see a fireman, police officer, or sports figure, and they say, "That's what I want to be when I grow up." The truth is, a lot of us have no idea what we want to be when we grow up. I've met people in their fifties who weren't sure they were doing what they really wanted to do.

The secret to finding what you want to do is finding, as early as possible, what you're good at and what you like to do. Just because you like to teach people how to do things doesn't mean you have to teach in a school. You can be a drill instructor, coach, personal trainer, or corporate trainer. There are lots of places outside of an elementary school, high school, or college where you can "teach" and work with students.

Part of finding out what it is you do or like means trying different things. Think of life like a buffet line. Sample a little of everything that looks interesting. You might not like it, but something you haven't tasted before might become your favorite food.

PAPERBOY

My first entrepreneurial experience was a success, not because I liked the job so much, but I did enjoy the money, and I learned some other really valuable things, too.

I was fourteen years old when I decided to follow in the footsteps of my big brother and make money on my terms. So I replied to an ad in the local newspaper for a position as a paperboy. I still remember the day the newspaper sales manager came by our house. He sat down at our kitchen table and began his spiel.

"Steven, do you have any friends who have a job?" he asked.

I replied, "Yes, I have a friend who works at Burger King."

He continued. "How much does he make per hour?"

"He makes three dollars and fifteen cents per hour," I answered.

"Well, Steve, you reached out to us at a perfect time. We recently expanded the newspaper route. Now we need more hardworking young men like yourself to seize this marvelous opportunity." He went on. "If you follow my process, I will teach you how you can make up to eight dollars per hour. And you won't have to work in a greasy restaurant or smell like hamburgers all day." He took out a notepad, pen, and calculator and proceeded to sell me on the opportunity of paperboy. He explained the process of working the paper route as if I had already accepted the position.

"Steve, the bundle of papers will be delivered to your doorstep every Thursday at four a.m.

"You'll prepare the newspapers for delivery. That will take you one hour.

"You'll run the route for approximately one hour, depending how fast you work.

"It'll take you another two hours collecting the subscription payments on Friday afternoon and Saturday morning.

"The average total subscriptions collected is sixty-four dollars. Of course, you have to send thirty-two dollars to *The Daily Sun* newspaper.

"That leaves you with thirty-two dollars for yourself!

"OK, now you do the math. How much did you make in four hours of work?"

I did the math in my head. "Eight dollars per hour," I answered. I was sold.

This was my first sales job. Not only did I learn the value of making my own money, but I learned the responsibility of managing and handling other people's money. That established the foundation for understanding the responsibility of being in a fiduciary position. Making money on my own terms also gave me a level of pride and self-confidence I hadn't had before. My first time out of the gate, I was bitten hard by the entrepreneurial bug. And for the next twenty years, I would continue to chase the feeling of financial freedom.

RENEGADES

My next turn in entrepreneurship came in a unique way. I always knew my way out would require something different of me. One of my first loves was art. I wanted to be an artist. It gave me an escape from reality. Unlike other people, I was able to create and live in this imaginary world. It helped me to tolerate some of the up and downs throughout my life. When I was frustrated or disappointed, I drew pieces of art. My class assignments, textbooks, and notes were filled with graffiti and characters. When I became disengaged with the lessons, I drifted into my imaginary world of art. Little did I know at the time that it would also turn into a business. I'd hoped it would, but I didn't realize the path creativity would lead me down.

This is another example of how you can sample your interests and hobbies and turn them into opportunities. Most of the time you won't stumble into something that's all laid out specifically for you. Pay attention to the things you enjoy, and take note of the things you don't.

My love for visual art expanded to another art form of expression: hip-hop. Once again, I was intrigued by the ability to express myself on my terms: when, where, and how I wanted to. Hip-hop had no formal methods of expression. All you needed was talent, turntables, and a microphone. It encompassed music, dance, visual art, and the entrepreneurship opportunity I desired. From the moment I was introduced to hip-hop, I wanted to become a producer. I pushed myself to learn all aspects of this industry, including writing, rapping, and producing.

Immediately, I had a desire to learn how to generate income from this art form. Here's where networking and connections came in handy. My older brother was a DJ. He and his crew would practice in the basement of our home. One night before they headed out to a gig, he left the microphone on. My cousin Will and I grabbed the mic and performed one of the songs we wrote. My brother and his friends were astonished by our talent. We knew we had something. Later that year, my brother Phil told my cousin and me, "I'm gonna put some money behind ya'll and push ya'll rap thing." Although this might sound a little weird to most of you, this is the way most rappers get their first opportunity to pursue their dream. Rappers start by pursuing their passion and their love for the art form, and then someone discovers them. We were lucky in that we knew people already in the industry. If you don't know anyone in the field where you're trying to break in, then start meeting them.

What you see in the movies about how people get their big breaks has only happened to a select few. Most inspiring music artists have a long, difficult journey. At that time, hip-hop was not a genre that major record labels were willing to invest in easily. So artists needed to build a "buzz," and in many cases, that meant they had to sell some records before an artists and repertoire (A&R) rep would even listen to their demo. Breaking into the industry isn't cheap. These artists had to have funding for studio time, engineering, professional mixing, and demo packaging. Most of the investors in inspiring hip-hop artists were street hustlers. Yet over the next couple of years, we were in the studio recording song after song because my brother believed in me and invested in me financially.

When we finally finished our demo, it was time to "shop it." After several meetings with A&R reps, we were getting frustrated with our dream. The truth is, Cleveland didn't have a big entertainment pool back then. And outside of the city, people didn't take Cleveland artists seriously because of the negative stigma surrounding the city.

We were fortunate that my uncle had a connection to a well-known record label executive who was responsible for the careers of several R&B artists in the 1970s and 1980s. After this executive heard our demo, he reached out to schedule a conference call. We were very excited; we thought this could be our big break. But what looks like a lucky break isn't always what it seems to be.

During that meeting, the executive gave us information that possibly was the turning point in each of our lives. He said, "I like your music. You guys are talented. But, what's selling right now is gangster rap. If you want to sell records, you have to be more hardcore. People want to hear about the hard life. They want you to be killers, dealers…you know what I mean. Make some hardcore songs, and we might be able to work something out."

The air went out of the room. We sat and looked at each other for what seemed like five minutes. I couldn't take it any longer. I grabbed the phone and replied, "Mr. G, I appreciate the advice. But we are not about that fake thug gangster rap. Our style is hip-hop. We have no intentions of exploiting our people and making light of the struggle. I'm sorry; we can't do that."

He responded, "I understand. If you want to sell records, this is what you have to do."

I knew that we had an opportunity. And I knew that this opportunity would've derailed us. It would have taken us away from our vision. Although we could've signed with a major label, it could've put us in a place of disappointment and hurt in the long run. So, we did the next best thing we could have—start our own record label. In 1993, we started SCR (Step City Records) and Renegade Music Group. My brother Phil was CEO, I was the VP, and Cousin Will was the featured artist of the group. This was my second entrepreneurial experience. I think I learned more by starting my own company than I would have signing under a music label.

During this experience as an independent record label owner and artist, I learned a lot about running a business. We had to negotiate agreements with local record stores to retail our music through consignment. We had to present our radio package to many radio stations in the Midwest. We finally struck a deal with a semiregional distribution company. There was a lot more learning than making money or gold records at that time.

Although we didn't go platinum or gold, we were exposed to thousands of people. That exposure introduced me to a lot of new of people and taught me to be comfortable doing it. I learned how to shake hands, talk to anyone about anything, and put other people (and myself) at ease with just a few words. I began to easily identify people who could help me reach the next level of success. I became a more likeable person, more approachable, and more of a "people person."

Exposure is great thing, but it can put your brand and intellectual property at risk. My experience as an independent artist showed me the importance of protecting my property. We had some of our music, production, and material stolen from us. Not everyone you meet is out to help, support, or build up your brand. There are people who see you as their meal ticket, their fast fortune, and worse. Knowing how to protect yourself and your brand is a huge part of being an entrepreneur. This ownership opportunity opened many doors for us, and it continues to open doors to this day. Nothing you do or learn in life is wasted. Everything has a value, and it provides an experience for you. It is our experiences that we learn from and that help us to become greater later down the line. It's important to make decisions based on what feels good to you. Your subconscious mind knows what your ambitions, goals, and passions are, and it will warn you if it's not in agreement with anything that could take you off your path.

3

MEETING MY MENTOR

*A mentor is someone who sees more talent and ability within you,
than you see in yourself, and then helps bring it out of you.*

~Bob Proctor

Many people meet their primary mentor as they grow up and get out into the world. I was fortunate enough to grow up with two of my mentors: my father and my brother. I grew up around semitrucks because my father was a truck driver. I spent many summers traveling around the country with my dad. He was my mentor, coach, and business partner. Going on the road with my father was something I enjoyed dearly, not only because I got a chance to see much of the Midwest, but also because it strengthened our relationship.

My brother was also my business mentor. He started his second company, which was a pressure washing business. He had contracts with several local trucking companies that I would later find resourceful for my business. Because of our relationships with the owners/operators, I decided that truckers would be my niche for one of my future businesses.

Over the next ten years, I would become a serial entrepreneur. I was addicted to the rush of starting and running my own business. My next entrepreneurial opportunity presented itself in the other art form I was in love with. I was selected to participate in a high school art program. I was a pretty decent visual artist. I used this gift as a tool to make my experience in school a lot more tolerable.

The purpose of this program was to help us master our skills and prepare our portfolio to enroll in an art university. The art director of the district happened to be the teacher for the program. He had an associate that was a franchisee of a large automobile tire retailer. The franchisee wanted an advertisement mural on the front of the tire shop, so the teacher selected a handful of the students in the program to do the mural for extra credit. It came out great. At that moment, I decided to start a sign company. In 1994, I started my sign company, Sign Language.

Because of father and brother's connection with truckers, I was *immediately* given the opportunity to start creating logos, murals, and lettering for many of the truckers my brother had cleaning contracts with. There's a lot to be said for networking and connections, and that was positive proof that networking is invaluable. I searched for trucks that had crooked or generic lettering when they brought them in to be cleaned. While in the presence of the owner, I pitched my services to him or her. It was almost a guaranteed sell. The most valuable lesson I learned from this business was how developing an "eye" for identifying opportunities can be profitable. Opportunities don't come up and slap you in the face or even knock on your head and announce themselves. You have to be on the lookout for them. There's a quote from Mark Twain that says, "The reason most people don't spot opportunity when they see it is that it comes wearing overalls and is disguised as work."

The men whose trucks had crooked lettering or no logos weren't thinking about lettering. They were not able to recognize the importance of branding. It was up to me to spot the opportunity to provide them with a service that would enhance their business. When you can find a solution to a problem or help someone with his or her business, that's almost always going to help grow your business.

KEEP ON TRUCKING

After seeing the success my father and brother were having with their new trucking business, I was inspired to start my own trucking company.

All the money I had was $2,500. Where could I find a truck for less than $2,000? The only person I knew who had an awesome ability to find cheap vehicles was my father. When I told my father that I wanted to start a trucking company, he immediately knew where the perfect truck was.

My dad had been saying for years that there was a big opportunity in trucking for someone to take advantage of: "hotshots." Sometimes, manufacturers have items that need to be shipped right away. In many of those cases, the items are too large, heavy, or awkward for same-day delivery companies like UPS. Hotshot trucking companies specialize in moving last-minute freight that weighs one thousand to ten thousand pounds. They usually have a much higher shipping rate than traditional trucking companies. What's really unique about this type of trucking company is you can start this business with a heavy-duty pickup truck and trailer or a midsize straight truck.

The truck my father had in mind was a 1975 U-Haul truck that a farmer was selling. My father saw the truck parked on the farm while he was delivering a load to a steel manufacturing company in rural Ohio. At first sight, this truck was in very bad shape. It is what farmers call a "yard mule." Farmers use them to transport hay, farming equipment, and other material around the farm. This truck was rusty, dented up, and just plain ugly. The truck probably hadn't see a paved road in at least ten years. It was perfect. The farmer was asking $2,500 for it. I used one of my father's salesman techniques; I counted out $1,800 in front of the farmer and placed it in his hand. I said, "I'll give you $1,800 for it." He agreed. That's all it took for me to officially start Cleveland Transport, my trucking company.

The next step was to come back and pick up the truck. There was only one problem: I didn't know how to drive a stick shift! The next day, my cousin and I came back to the farm to pick the truck up. I followed my cousin as he was driving the truck back to Cleveland. The truck was blowing huge clouds of black smoke, backfiring, and drifting from lane to lane. Passerby were looking and laughing at this "dinosaur" crawling its way down the busy highway, but I was not embarrassed. In fact, I was proud. See, I've been resurrecting clunkers for years. Every car I've owned to this point had been in bad condition when I purchased it. I saw the potential in this truck. The next step was to get it up to par. Over the next month, I tuned the engine, adjusted the brakes, and spray-painted the entire truck.

Once the truck was painted and ready to roll, the next step was to put it to work. I started promoting my trucking business the only way I knew how: guerilla marketing. I created fifty flyers and went door-to-door of every small machine shop I could find. One of the shops I stopped by was a small, family-owned erecting company. It was a dark, grungy warehouse with several young men inside who were welding very large pieces of steel. I went to the front office to hand my flyer to a manager. I was greeted by a very big guy who told me he was one of the owners. After looking at my flyer, he called his dad over to check it out. His father asked me if the truck was outside. I replied, "Yes sir." Hugh Jr. and his father came outside to inspect my truck. After exchanging some words in their native language, possibly Greek, Hugh said, "Are you available tomorrow? We have some work for you." The family started using my trucking company to haul equipment and materials to jobsites. Now I really was in business!

WIDE WORLD

After returning from delivering some welding equipment, I walked into Hugh's office with my trip log. Hugh Sr. walked up to me and said, "Steve, you ever thought about starting an escort service?"

Thinking he was implying adult services, I replied, "Huh, I'm not into that, sir."

He laughed and clarified: "No, no...you know, the guys you see on the highway with wide load signs and flags on their cars."

"OK, I know what you're talking about," I responded.

Hugh Sr. said, "Follow me."

I followed him to the side of the warehouse to a large lot where they stored steel and materials. He began to explain what they did in more detail. "We're an erecting company. We build steel structures for construction companies. One of our largest contracts is with a national pharmacy brand. We recently signed a contract with a contractor that's building an automated warehouse for a furniture company. This is going to be the warehouse of the future! It will be a distribution center run by robots! The furniture will be stored at this location in bins, and when an order is placed, the robot forklift will roll directly to the rack, pick it up, and bring it down to be loaded on the delivery truck." He went on to state that the contractor will need over a thousand of these racks to build the facility. The Department of Transportation requires a licensed escort vehicle to trail these oversized loads. He advised me that if I got licensed in Ohio, Pennsylvania, and New York, he would be able to use me. There was another door of opportunity that just opened up. This is when I experienced my fifth entrepreneurial journey. I started my highway escort service, Wide World Transport Service.

4

THE FIRST STEP

I am learning to trust God and His plan for my life and the journey I'm on.

~Steven D. Compton

I hate change. My whole life up to this point had been full of inconsistencies and change. I think my drive for entrepreneurship was fueled by the desire to control my outcome.

Like most people, when change occurs, I get frightened. But I've become so accustomed to it that it now seems like second nature. I now believe that I thrived on change. Every two years, I found myself taking on another business venture. It was easy to take on new business opportunities because I personally funded them. I was not fortunate enough at that time to get a line of credit at a bank or have an investor. I couldn't borrow money from any family members because they didn't have it to loan me. My early businesses were funded from money I saved up.

In the case of my trucking company, I literally used a tax return refund to purchase a 1975 U-Haul truck. My first insurance agency was funded by money I saved while working as a commission-only insurance agent for another agency owner.

Some people think that once you start your own business, you're totally in charge and that things just fall into place for you. That's not true. I received a lot of pushback. In the early years, my family didn't think I should have wasted my time pursuing the music business, but I did it anyway. Not everyone wanted to buy the records I was selling, and money was tight. That's the life of the entrepreneur. But things can also get personal, and that can hurt.

When I decided to start my insurance agency, I had to interview with a variety of sales managers. I was told by three different sales managers that I had an excellent track record in sales. But they were concerned that I lacked the business sense to run a business. Hearing that kind of bothered me. For a long time, my confidence in my ability to be a successful entrepreneur was low. I thought my lack of a formal education was going to limit me. Now, my insurance agency is in the top 1 percent in the country for the insurance carrier I represent. It took a while, but I learned the most important thing about entrepreneurship that any entrepreneur should know: success isn't based on your education, background, financial smarts, or all of the things people say you have to have to succeed. It's based on how much you want it and how hard you are willing to work to get it. You don't have to be the best, the most talented, or the sharpest tool in the box. You just have to be willing to have a vision and work for it. Persistence trumps talent every time. There are a lot of talented, intelligent people out there, but if they aren't willing to show up, do the work, and be there when no one else wants to be, they won't succeed.

It helps if you have people around you that believe in you and support you. It can be a teacher, mentor, friend, or if you're lucky, your family. My family has become very supportive over the years; I suppose they knew that the alternative to my new business was my going back to the streets or selling drugs. My father was always especially supportive. I believe he didn't want me to follow his footsteps and become a truck driver.

The negativity about my business didn't start until I started interacting with "educated" people in corporate America. It seemed like many of the managers, supervisors in the insurance industry did not think I had enough formal education and prestige to transition into professional sales.

I remember when I visited an insurance agency owner to inquiry about the process of becoming an agent, he belittled me by pointing out my clothes were too shabby, I need to shave, and I was too unpolished to be an agent. The same type ridicule continued later when I opened my own insurance agency. When I started getting pushback from them, I had some close friends suggest I get a corporate sales job after my first insurance agency failed. I failed a lot, but I never felt defeated.

Now that I am experiencing success, most of my current associates don't know all the things I did in the past, including my experience in drug dealing. So I'm here to tell you that many people have rough starts and have to work through or with failures. That's just a part of being an entrepreneur. If it was easy, everyone would be doing it. You have to want the lifestyle or be able to thrive within the lifestyle, which means working hard and dealing with change to cope with negative and failure that might arise. It's not for everyone. Starting a business, living on commission only, and not having a guaranteed paycheck has never been an issue for me. In fact, I prefer that over the restrictions of a job. If you aren't comfortable with uncertainty and not knowing what's going to happen next and whether you're going to succeed or fail, then being an entrepreneur might not be the best option for you. If you want success badly enough, you will learn to live with uncertainty and change. You're the only one who can make that decision. I am now committed to learning to love change, and I entered a whole new world, one where whether I fail or succeed will be based on my faith, my choices, and my personal decisions. For that, I am willing to take the risk.

5

THE GAME

I'm not telling you it's going to be easy.
I'm telling you it's going to be worth it.

~Steven D. Compton

Like the saying goes, "We're born alone and we die alone, but if you're lucky enough to find family and friends in between, you're doing well."

I was one of the lucky ones. When I moved to Atlanta, most of my support came from friends. Although most of my family and friends back in Cleveland didn't understand what it took to start a business, they believed in me. They just didn't have the knowledge of where to begin or what to tell me about getting started. Every business I started, I did by doing my own research.

Don't let not having supportive family or friends stop you from starting. I had the emotional support from people close to me, but when it came to learning how to run a business, other business owners were the best sources of advice for me.

Throughout the years as an insurance agency owner, I met hundreds of insurance professionals. Many of us supported one another, and we shared ideas and resources regularly. Especially being African American insurance agency owners (making up less than 5 percent of the industry), we rely on one another. Unfortunately, I've seen the vast majority of African American insurance agency owners go out of business for reasons I think could have been avoided. This is one reason I wrote this book. You have to surround yourself around other professionals in the industry you're looking to pursue so that you are aware of obstacles that might come your way.

Anytime someone says, "drug dealer," people immediately think of television or the movies, and all the big-time, life of crime stereotypes. That wasn't me. I wasn't a big-time drug dealer. I was really just supporting my own habit and making a couple thousand a month off of selling drugs. The reason I wasn't dealing bigger deals was I didn't have to. I had other businesses and opportunities going for me at the time. Opportunity was all around me, and most of it was legal. What I learned from selling drugs was how to be an entrepreneur. It was a combination of selling drugs, being around big-time drug dealers, and running these "hustles" that my small business opportunities gave me all I needed to know about real entrepreneurship.

The drug game really taught me that I, all the young men I was involved with, and those I knew who were successful drug dealers also had the savvy to be legitimate businessmen. It was never the drugs that made them "rich." It was the risk. It was their ability to negotiate. They developed the ability to form syndicates and distributors to get their product out. Some of them had intricate systems around how customers would purchase product from them.

The reason people fail as drug dealers has nothing to do with the "business" part of the drug business; it's because drug dealing is immoral, and there is no trust and loyalty. People might laugh at that statement, but integrity, trust, and loyalty are the foundations of any successful business. Without those characteristics, any business, legal or not, is no different than the drug dealer, scam artist, crook, or thief.

Just like any legal product, if your objective to sell a product doesn't add value to someone's life, you won't be in business long.

WHAT DRUG DEALING TAUGHT ME ABOUT BUSINESS

Weigh your risks. Honestly, the biggest lesson I learned from drug dealing was to weigh the risks and the rewards. When I get frustrated or start to lose motivation in my business, I think back to the days I risked my life and freedom for a couple hundred dollars. And now, I can shake a few hands, shuffle a few papers, stroke a few keys on the keyboard, and make more than a couple hundred dollars—often a few thousand dollars. I thank God for the transformation.

Location, location, location. That's normally the mantra of realtors, but location was an important part of the drug-selling business. You had to be where people could find you and where it was easy for people to contact you and get your product. But the smart ones (really not that smart if they chose this career) had guaranteed clientele.

Guaranteed clientele. Drugs do for the dealer what the entrepreneur has to figure out how to do for him- or herself: guarantee return customers and clientele. Drugs are addicting. When people find a supplier or dealer where they can get what need and the quality is good, and they're addicted, they keep going back to that same source. When you're an entrepreneur, you're not likely to be able to rely on addiction to keep your customers coming back time after time. You need to figure out a way to entice them with other things, like great customer service, value, a solid product, and a professional relationship that lets them know you really care about them. It cost less money and time to keep a satisfied customer than it does to go out and find new customers. I learned I can't rely on the product itself to keep people returning. I have to do more.

6

F.E.A.R.

F.E.A.R. is focusing on every alternative result.

~Steven D. Compton

My mother died from a short battle with breast cancer when I was eight years old. She left behind my big brother, Phil, my big sister, Chris, my father, and me. My siblings are much older than me, so they moved out on their own a few years after she passed. My father raised me alone. I grew up in a bachelor pad. My dad was a truck driver. He would leave home every morning at 4:00 a.m. He wouldn't return until 8:00 p.m. that evening. That left me to pretty much take care of myself. I was the epitome of a latchkey kid. Although my dad wasn't a typical dad, he did the best he could. We just didn't have much to work with. I was in a better situation than many children. That's not to say I had an easy childhood, because I didn't. It was riddled with fears that a child shouldn't have to have.

My father was loving father, but he was a compulsive gambler. He spent a large portion of his weekly check at the horse track, placing bets. I watched my father work very hard during the week driving trucks, and I saw him spend it just as quickly as he made it.

Considering Cleveland is known for having blizzards, his job was dangerous. He would go on the road regardless of the weather conditions. One of my biggest fears was that he would not return home. I suffered from insomnia through most of my early life because I couldn't sleep thinking about him being on the road. I never received professional help. My first attempt to self-medicate was taking over-the-counter sleeping pills. I still couldn't sleep. It wasn't until I started smoking marijuana when I was eighteen years old that I got my first good sleep. That was also when I got involved in selling drugs. I used marijuana and drank alcohol every day over a ten-year period.

We were evicted many times during my early childhood years. I had a constant fear of moving. One of my earliest memories of being evicted was when I was four years old. We lost our beautiful home in the Heights. I remember a sheriff standing in front of our house with his 0.38 special as our stuff was being put out on the front lawn.

The thing about fears, particularly childhood fears, is that they always stay with you. It's how our brains work. Fear helps us make associations that keep us from harm. Fear is a survival mechanism. Even if we don't consciously recognize something that might harm us, our bodies will spot the signs and alert us with feelings of anxiety or even terror.

If a drug deal goes bad, a bully punches you, or a potential client rejects you, your brain will remember everything about the encounter and file it away as a threat. Whether your childhood bully was a big, ugly dude or a skinny weasel, people who remind you of him or her will become people you have a hard time trusting, no matter how trustworthy they are. When something or someone imprints on your mind as a threat, then the next time you encounter those same triggers, you'll react with fear, even if the situation is safe. When we learn from fear, we learn quickly. Fear learning is powerful and long-lasting. Think back to your childhood. Chances are that your earliest memory is an event connected to fear.

Not meeting the standard of my colleagues is a fear I've struggled with until this day. Many of my schoolmates from high school went to college. I didn't do well academically in school. I was just bored and distracted by life. I was a C student, or "see" student. I was just trying to *see* my way through. I didn't fully apply myself, and I didn't have the proper support system at home. I knew in my heart that I wanted to be an artist (music and visual). Initially, I didn't see why pursuing a degree in higher education would help me fulfill this dream. I decided to give college a chance and completed one year at Cleveland State. Unfortunately, I had the same results I received in high school: low grades, no support system, and no connection with college being a part of my career path. I dropped out. That experience created the fear of not being qualified enough to be successful that stayed with me for the rest of my life. When those sales managers questioned my business skills, it brought up a constant reminder that I did not complete my degree.

I carried a lot of bad habits into my adulthood: drinking, smoking, and partying. I was headed down a dark path. All the businesses I started failed. It felt like everything I started never fully became what I envisioned. I was on an emotional and financial roller coaster. Instead of addressing the real issues in my life, I covered them up by getting high. It wasn't until I moved to Atlanta in 2001 that my life started to change in a positive direction. I moved to Atlanta for a new life, and that's what I found. I moved there with only $400 in my pocket. My belongings were all in garbage bags. I moved in with my sister and slept on her floor for two months. I was determined to make a path for my life.

When you go looking for something different, it's funny how you eventually find it. And you don't always find it in the places you'd think. I found my new life in a Christian church in Atlanta. For two entire years, I did nothing but work, go to church, and read my Bible. I was in church six days a week. Although some of the beliefs were a bit radical and edgy, that consecration period was like a cleansing for me.

During that time, I stopped smoking marijuana, stopped partying, and became very focused. For the first time, I included God in my life and on my journey toward success. With my newfound beliefs, I discovered that God not only wants us spiritually sound but physically, mentally, and financially sound.

I had a solid foundation from my past for how to start and run a business, but now I also had spiritual motivation to pursue my passion of entrepreneurship. I saw that even the prosperity message in some charismatic Christian churches have been plagued with images of false success. Now, I'm focused on pleasing God through living for him, and I focus on adding value to others. Regardless of whether it's dealing drugs or seeking fortune through twisting Bible principles, if our sole focus or idea of "success" equates to riches, stardom, or material things, it's false success. I know that's hard for many people to accept, but I urge you to take time to step back and think about it. What matters most comes from the heart. True success is being able to love God, others, and ourselves.

The kind of love the Bible talks about isn't the same kind of love we see in movies or on television. It's not something we can do on our own. But when we learn to love and trust God to show us how to love, that is true success.

OVERCOMING FEAR

I still shake my head when I hear people talk about "how hard" life and being an entrepreneur is. I tell them that following God doesn't make life easier. It just gives you the strength to deal with the hard times. If you look at the heroes in the Bible, they didn't have it easy. In fact, they had it harder than most!

Joseph was betrayed by his own brothers! All eleven of them! He was beaten and thrown into a pit to die. God had other plans for him, and so his brothers ended up selling him to slave traders instead. He eventually ended up as a slave to one of Pharaoh's guards, Potiphar.

Moses didn't have an easy start, either. Pharaoh was out to kill all newborn male Israelites so they would never grow up and fight against him. Rather than drown her son, Moses's own mother put him in a basket into a river full of crocodiles, hippopotamuses, and other creatures that could kill and eat him. But God had other plans for Moses, who was then rescued by Pharaoh's daughter. He ended up being raised and educated as royalty in an Egyptian household. He became a younger brother to Rameses II, the future pharaoh of Egypt!

God gives us the strength to get through life. He has a plan for you, even if you can't see it. I imagine Moses often asked God what He envisioned for him! The secret to success is not to focus on where you are, how bad you have it, who has betrayed you, or how broke you are. The secret is to focus on your passion, purpose, and on God's plan for your life.

I've been very discouraged throughout my life. I can't count the times I thought all was lost or that I'd hit a dead end. When I felt discouraged, I prayed. My motivation was fueled by my determination to prove the naysayers wrong. Lots of people, more than I want to remember, thought I would become a basket case when my mother died. They didn't think my father had the ability to raise me and continue to drive trucks. They were wrong. I learned many of the skills of self-sufficiency during those times.

Many thought I would get locked up for selling drugs, or even worse, become a user. I never got locked up, although I did use for a while, but with the grace of God, I stopped. My drug dealing was illegal, but God used it to teach me about entrepreneurship. King David was an adulterer and a murderer, yet God used those sins to turn his life around and into good.

I was motivated by proving the Devil was wrong about me being another lost soul wandering around with no purpose. The sales managers that told me to my face that I was not good enough to be a businessman weren't a deterrent, but a challenge. I wanted to prove them wrong about how good I was and how good I could be, and I did. A college professor at Cleveland State once told me, "You're not going to amount to shit!" I wanted to prove him wrong, and I did.

I wanted to win and to succeed in my life for every one of my family members back in Cleveland who might be discouraged or defeated and for the young men who think they have to choose a life in the streets. My message to you right now is to not let the negativity in your life, or the people attacking, bullying, or telling you that you can't do it, shape your future. If I can turn my life around, you can, too.

When you put your trust in God, He will turn the worst things in your life into good. He did it with everyone in the Bible. He did it for me, and He'll do it for you, too. Trust Him.

7

THE COMMISSION

The journey is the reward.

~Old Chinese Proverb

When my big brother Phil, my cousin Will, and I started our own record label after being rejected by several major record labels, it was the first time I felt the rush of real success. Hearing our music on the radio gave me a sense that we'd made it, we were special, and we created something that no one could take away from us.

Like most entrepreneurs and creative types, successful or not, I'm addicted to that rush. By rush, I mean the thrill of creating a business and the fear of losing a business. That tension of creating, selling, building, and working hard at a business and not knowing what's going to happen creates an adrenaline rush that can't be explained. You're really competing against the odds of failure. And to beat it feels great. It wasn't just music that gave me that rush. Sales did, too.

When I was a commission-only sales producer, my first commission check was $1,500 for a month's worth of sales. My mentor and boss Mel told me, "Don't ever let me write you another check this small!"

I was thinking, "This is small? Do you know how hard I had to work at my last job to make $1,500?"

And that was the day I knew sales was what I wanted to do.

When I got into the insurance business in 2003, I couldn't believe how much money insurance agents made. Insurance was also my first opportunity to interact with corporate America. The same place that I was afraid that my lack of formal education would prevent me from getting to, and the place sales managers told me I would never achieve, drew me in. I was good at selling, and it had nothing to do with a formal education. It had everything to do with my ability to connect with people. When I realized I was good at what I did from that point on, all I wanted to do was sales. I considered sales as the back door to corporate America.

I was doing business with CEOs, presidents, VPs, and MBAs, and I knew more about insurance than they did. That motivated me even more. I was determined to become an insurance expert. So I studied policy contracts, attended several sales seminars, and networked with high-performing insurance agents. I figured out why sales was so lucrative. Salespeople can do something that all the corporate heads can't; they can sell. If you can sell their product, they'll pay you a lot of money. And I could sell. From that first $1,500 check on, I continued to make more and more in commissions. I knew I was a success because I was making money, but the first time I felt that I'd arrived was when I got my first $30,000 commission check. I know, it sounds like I'm chasing the money, something I said isn't true success. What I was chasing wasn't the money. The money was a by-product of true success—of following God's plan for my life and of treating my customers with respect, honesty, loyalty, and the best customer service I have to offer.

True success, for me, was proving to myself, my friends, family, and all those strangers, teachers, and businessmen who never believed in me that I was so much more than what they saw in me. God saw something different. I saw something different, and when I made improving myself, my life, and who I was to become the goal of my life, success followed. It sounds counterintuitive. If you're emotionally needy, no one wants to be around you. When you become emotionally confident, and you don't need anyone to support you, everyone wants to be around you.

When I was desperately looking for financial success, I couldn't find it. When I stopped looking for financial success and started focusing on being the best person I could be and on following God and my faith, the financial success appeared. Money is good. I won't argue about that.

But the best feeling I've had is having one of the fastest-growing agencies in the country. Averaging 300 percent more monthly sales than most retail agencies says more than I'm making it financially. It says I'm the person God intended me to be. My true success is as a person, as a believer. The money is icing on the cake, as they say.

Instead of being told, "You don't have what it takes to be a successful businessman or salesman," I now receive calls from other insurance agency owners all over the country asking, "How are you able to be so successful in this business?" Other people may measure my success by my bank account, but I measure it by who I have become, by how far I've come, and by where I'm going.

Remember I said I'm a serial entrepreneur? I see opportunities when they present themselves. I noticed that I was asked that question so much that I decided to start a sales training and agency coaching business.

It's funny how the enemy attacks you in the very area God wants to use you. More on that in the next chapter.

8

MOTIVATION

Sometimes, proving to others that they're wrong about you, can be more motivating than proving your right to those that doubt you.

~Steven D. Compton

It's funny how the enemy attacks you in the very area God wants to use you. We tend to think that once we "make it," get to the top of our industry, or begin to be successful, respected, or in demand from others for our expertise, that things get easier for us. People assume everyone likes us or treats us well. I will be the first person to tell you that none of that is true. In fact, the closer you get to the top of the ladder, the more difficulty, spiritual attacks, and issues you'll find yourself having.

This is true for all mankind. If you go back and look at the life Moses had, you'll see that even God's appointed and anointed suffered! A lot of ministers and people I've met over the years love to point out that Moses argued with God over being chosen to lead God's people out of Egypt. The sermons I've heard on this topic generally revolve around his reluctance, his fear, and his not being willing to follow God. As an entrepreneur, I have another perspective on what might have been going through Moses's mind.

Remember, Moses was raised in Pharaoh's house. He was raised as a prince, one of the highest offices in the land—just shy of Pharaoh himself. Moses was schooled in business, success, wealth, power, and all the trappings of success. I think he knew more than just how to run a country and that he saw firsthand how jealous, devious, untrustworthy, greedy, and backstabbing people can be when they're around money, fame, and fortune. I don't think he told God he wasn't the best person to lead the people out of Egypt because he was shy or not a good public speaker. I think Moses struggled with knowing he didn't know how to deal with the drama, stress, and battles that come along with being a leader. He knew how the people would react once they were out of Egypt and wandering in the desert. I think Moses tried to get out being God's leader because he had seen how even God-fearing, God-worshipping people can be.

Remember, the journey to the promised land should have taken Moses and the two-million-plus people he was leading only about two to four weeks to make. Yet it took forty years! And Moses never actually got to go into the promised land, and neither did most of the people who left Egypt. Why? Drama. Disobedience. Distrust.

When you're a leader or the best or most successful at anything you do, prepare for an ongoing spiritual, emotional, and even physical battle. When you're at the top of your game, even if you're just a big fish in a small pond, haters are going to hate.

While Moses got to "see God" and had a lot of mountaintop experiences and communication with God over that forty years his leadership was still challenged by his followers. He parted the Red Sea, brought water out of a rock in the desert, and turned a staff into a snake and then back into a staff. Look at all the miracles and acts he performed. God wrote on stone with His finger and handed the Ten Commandments to Moses to take back to the people. Moses spent so much time with God that his face literally glowed like the sun when he came down from the mountain. Big opportunities bring big resistance and battles, though. You and I are no different. We have that mountaintop experience, and then things blow up or get negative. We begin to wonder and even doubt if we're really in the place God wants us. That's normal. It's how God develops us, but it's rarely fun. It just is. Learning to deal with it when it happens is important if you want to continue to be a success.

Like I mentioned earlier in the book, I receive calls from insurance agents all over the country asking for my advice. I try to help them as much as I can. And they are so grateful for the assistance. But there are a few agency owners who question my success. During one incident, a tenured insurance agent asked me, "Did your business mentor set your business up?" He asked that as if I didn't have the capabilities to start my business or do as well as I was on my own.

To this day, I still have not received recognition from many of my colleagues. Many people wouldn't even think twice about that, but because of my struggles to get to where I am, I am still very much aware that I am still fighting to get the acknowledgment I want.

Recently, another insurance agency owner asked me, "Now that the bonuses have gone away, are you going to be able to keep doing all that business?" Other top-producing agents are never asked this type of question. Why me? I'm not sure. Instead of questioning whether other top producers will be able to keep up, they are asked, "Can you tell me how you're able to write so much business, even when bonuses have gone away?"

One question they ask me comes from a doubt that I'm truly capable, or it comes from a belief that my success was somehow some sort of fluke or luck and not a result of my talents, abilities, and skills. When you ask, "How are you able to be a success in the face of the loss of bonuses?" you're telling the agent you're impressed and curious. It's a small difference, but it matters. Satan can use that doubt to attack me if I let him.

What I've learned from this is that you can tell someone's heart from how they communicate and what they communicate to you. The people who respect you and admire your success ask for advice. The people who question your success don't respect you, and it shows in their comments and actions and the way they talk to and about you. In fact, they believe your success is a fluke, or they want it to be. They are anticipating your failure and the smugness they'll feel when you fall. I used to get frustrated with "haters." But now I know what's behind the hating on one's successes. It's important you understand this, too, or you'll fall victim to the Devil's attack when these haters start hating on you.

People attack us, hate on us, or try to sabotage us because they think our success somehow threatens theirs.

There's an old story about how a martial arts teacher dealt with this issue. He drew two lines on a chalkboard: one short, one a bit longer. He put the names of the students in his class next to the shorter line and a well-known opponent's name next to the longer line. Then he asked them how they could make their opponent's line shorter. One student used the eraser to cut off the end of the opponent's line, and then there was another scribble on the line, distorting it. On and on they went, attacking the opponent's line. Finally, the teacher stopped them and told them they were all wrong.

"What is the answer then?" one student said. The teacher said nothing, but he picked up the chalk and made the line next to the student's names longer.

"We can't control others' successes," he said. "We can only control our own."

When people attack us, it's usually because they are unable to realize or materialize their own potential. They usually have a lack of support in their own lives, or they think if they destroy you, they will have a clear shot at the success they think you control. If people attack you, they may be competing against you, but not in a healthy way. Somewhere along the line, they learned a scarcity mentality. They believe there's honestly not enough success to go around.

The fast food industry understands this concept, but in small towns, many small businesses or diners don't. In small towns, you'll have several people who want to start a bakery, restaurant, or diner, but they won't. They'll say, "Well, Fred already has a burger place, and I don't want to take away his business" (as though they think they're so much better than Fred that their business would hurt his!).

However, if you look around any place where there's one fast food restaurant, there are almost always three or four other restaurants. Rather than competing with one another, they actually attract more customers.

Why? It's called being a restaurant destination or a business destination. People who only visit an area because of one restaurant won't visit the area unless they specifically want to go to that restaurant. But when you have several places offering different food, they actually attract more people. It's why malls are so popular. People like variety.

There is plenty to go around. We don't worry about there being enough air to breathe or sunlight to light up our days, do we? Why not? The same is true of success. There's plenty to go around. You just have to work at it. The people who believe in a scarcity of success don't want to work at it.

I speak to everyone. I love people. And I really love people in business (entrepreneurs). If I ever encountered an environment where entrepreneurs avoid speaking to me, they usually fall in this category of scarcity mentality. They are convinced that I'm a competitor there to take something away from them. There's only so much success, and when it's gone, it's gone! That's not true, and real entrepreneurs know it!

The enemy's job is to make people believe that in order to achieve true success, you must not only be better than others, but you can't let anyone else learn, grow, or become successful him- or herself. Haters believe there is not enough room at the top for everyone. They tell us, "It's lonely at the top" to reinforce that scarcity mentality.

Chances are, if you're lonely at the top, you are probably a hater. You chose not to share your successes with others. You chose not to bring others with you. True success is more about helping others than helping yourself. Others are concerned that another person experiencing success will somehow limit their own chances of achieving their dream.

And haters believe that if there is someone less educated, articulate, and privileged than them who is experiencing success then he's got to be doing something wrong. Because you surely can't be doing worse than someone beneath you. Haters consider your status, creed, and accolades, and compare them with their own. What they don't know is the very person they're prejudging might just have the secret of true success.

They can't open their minds long enough to let the thought in that that person could give them the insight that might change their world. I feel sorry for them. So many of them throw or turn away the very insights, help, and advice they could learn and grow from. It's their mind-sets, their hardened hearts, and their fear that holds them back.

In spite of the haters, I love helping entrepreneurs because I know what's really going on behind closed doors. I know what is taking place to make them able to pay their employees, pay rent, keep the lights on, and not to mention, take care of their families.

Division among small business owners has limited their success, and they don't even realize it. I once saw a cartoon illustration of what hell is like. It was a picture of people sitting a table with super long spoons strapped to one hand and a long pole with a glass of ice water on the other. There was an abundance of food on the table, a feast actually, but the spoons were so long that the people couldn't get the food from the table into their mouths, so they were starving. And they couldn't get the glasses to their mouths to drink, so they were parched as well. That was hell. The only thing different about heaven was that in heaven, people learned to feed one another! They used their spoons to feed their neighbors and give them a drink. Everyone was fed, happy, and content. Life is like that, too. When we feed one another, we all benefit. There is enough to go around. The scarcity belief is from the Devil.

I believe there's power in sharing, in caring, and in unity. So I've decided to dedicate my life to empowering entrepreneurs. I started another company called the Profit Package to do just that. The Profit Package is an information brand that promotes and creates info products designed to educate, empower, and encourage entrepreneurs. I know what frustrations they have. And for many of them, the source of the result they're getting is fear, division, and an unawareness of their potential. They are so consumed with the fear that someone is going to take away the little they do have that they clutch everything to themselves. This spirit and sense of lack and scarcity, and their desperation about losing everything, drives away customers and business. If it's not the fear that a so-called competitor might be the one responsible for the depletion of their great empire that grips them, it's the fear that they might have to return to that dead-end job they once held, back in corporate America. Or, in my case, back on the streets.

A lot of this goes back to the definition of success that we have. Small business owners have been convinced that they're not successful because they aren't multimillionaires. They believe that because they are not in the top 20 percent of performers of their industry, they are failures.

Believing the lie of false success, that you have to be rich and have a huge bank balance, has caused millions of business owners to prematurely shut their businesses down. It's sad.

Division among small business owners is a deadly poison to true success. It stunts growth, it promotes selfishness and strife, and it creates isolation. Ultimately, it leads to death. Death of a dream and vision. Look at the word itself: *di-vision...die-vision.*

Remember the table illustration, the spoons, and the difference between heaven and hell? Collaboration with others is encouraging, empowering, and, like any other relationship in which we're generous with others, it's healthy.

A large part of my successes in my personal life, business, and relationships, are a result of the support of other entrepreneurs. Competition can be healthy, especially for salespeople. But it can easily turn into envy and comparison.

When you leave the path of God-inspired passion, purpose, and plan, you'll find yourself comparing your achievements to those of others. And you'll begin to adopt a version of success based on what others have accomplished—that's false success.

Don't think I'm holier than thou and am criticizing any of you about this. I know about jealousy, envy, hatred, and the scarcity mentality because it's something I struggled with myself. I wasn't a hater of others' success by any means. But I was very self-conscious, both personally and professionally.

WHY HATERS HATE

A lot of people will hate the haters. It's natural to attack the people who attack us. What many people don't know is that's exactly why Jesus Christ told us to love those who hate us and treat us badly.

I think that whole "love your enemies as yourself" is one of the hardest commandments in the Bible to follow. It's certainly been challenging to me on more than one occasion. I just couldn't see what God saw in some people. How could anyone love some of these people? Then He showed me some things.

The source of hating on others can best described as low self-esteem. It's an outward reaction to some unresolved issues within. When people don't like or feel good about themselves, they may take it out on others. Studies show that many school and workplace bullies are bullied, beaten, and abused at home—not all of them, but a lot of them. When you can't fight back or change your own shortcomings, fears, and failures, you focus on the shortcomings of others so you don't have to think about your own. After a while, you even forget you have shortcomings because you have learned to ignore or deny them. Adult bullying (hating) is very similar to what bullies struggle with in grade school.

I was a chubby kid my whole life. I didn't have an athletic bone in my body. I was very self-conscious about it. I knew that I couldn't change who God made me. If I gave in to the idea that my uniqueness was a weakness, it would be very hard to overcome low self-esteem. So I decided to beat the system by becoming friends with everyone. That didn't keep me from being attacked by the bullies. My friendships help me cope with the fact that some people didn't like me, and they made me realize that "real" friends accept you for who you are.

I learned later in life that the comedian Jim Carrey and his family lived in a Volkswagen van when he was growing up. His self-esteem wasn't so great, either. He used humor to keep the bullies at bay. Like me, he befriended everyone, and he made them laugh. When people are laughing and having a good time, they're much less likely to notice you're homeless (like Carrey was), fat, ugly, short, awkward, shy, or just different.

Another tactic I used against low self-esteem and bullies was using my talents, skills, and abilities to outperform the haters. I was a very good artist. I used art as an edge against what I considered my handicap. I knew if I kept people in awe of my work, they wouldn't have time to focus on my weight. And it worked.

Most of us grow out of the many awkward phases of our childhood, but those memories and fears never really go completely away. They're replaced by what psychologists call the "fraud factor." While we may be hugely successful and truly talented and capable at whatever it is we're doing, we feel like we're "frauds" because that old, low self-esteem and our childhood demons—our weight, looks, hair, lack of athletic ability, shyness—are still there, still whispering (with the help of the Devil): "You're not good enough, smart enough, talented enough, or worthy of success." And when we listen to that voice inside us, it's no wonder we feel like frauds!

In many ways, I'm still that chubby kid struggling with self-consciousness and using my entrepreneurial drive as a mask. Some part of me tells me that if I do well in business, people might not notice my size and my lack of formal education.

What I realized over the years was that it wasn't my art, my brief music career, or my businesses that people were attracted to—it was me. People genuinely want to be around people that care for them, that have a genuine interest in the things that interest them, and who want them to succeed.

This is the reason I put my trust and faith in Christ. Christ embodied this idea that doing for others is more important than focusing on your own needs. He believed in that ideology to the point that he gave his life so others could receive "true success." Love conquers hate; it drives hate from your presence. Love is unity. Love doesn't run a race against people; it runs with people. Love is the source of the true success. It will keep you grounded in your passion, purpose, and plan, regardless if it seems like it's not doing as well as others around. When you abandon love, you abandon the plan for your life. And you'll find yourself right back to pursuing false success. Success can be just as deadly as failure.

Sometimes, when I see the reports of what I have achieved, they scare me. The fear of losing momentum and of not being as good as my best quarter begins to creep in. The thought of the struggles and failures I've experienced in the past comes out of hiding. It sticks its devilish head out from my past and reminds me: "I'm not gone yet!"

If you let it, failure will become an evil, lurking shadow waiting for his chance to crush your dreams rather than an opportunity to learn, grow, advance, and succeed.

If you fear failure, you'll institute *die-vision*, which will lead you to isolation and defeat. I have to remind myself that true success is the Creator's plan for those who align their passion, purpose, and plan with righteousness. And true success is a promise for those who commit to pursue integrity, faith, and the desire to add value to others.

An overflow of success creates a blessing for others and builds your legacy, and it encourages others to pursue their passion, purpose, and plan. True success is not riches, fame, or material things. Those things may come along as a result of pursuing true success, but they were never meant to be the focus or measure of success.

Failure, and I mean failing and giving up entirely, is not an option, not because of my determination to succeed. It's because of my determination to please the Creator by pursuing my passion of helping others, fulfilling my purpose of empowering others, and following my plan as an entrepreneur that will position me to receive His promises of prosperity and true success.

I believe that God's plan for everyone is to glorify Him. Regardless of your faith, God wants you to follow the "Golden Rule"—do unto others as you would have them do unto you—even when they hate you, do evil against you, bully you, and attack you.

Everyone wins when we adopt the idea of adding value to the lives of others. Passion is the burning desire to pursue a vision, purpose is the reason you're committing to a vision, and the plan is the detailed process to fulfilling that vision.

This journey of mine is what I call practicing true success. As you achieve goals within your passion, purpose, and plan, you're actually practicing success. The more you achieve, the more success you experience. It's not until you've completed *all* aspects of your passion, purpose, and plan that you become successful. You'll see successes along the way, and if you're in God's will, you'll recognize the work He's doing in you. I don't use the word successful lightly because I believe you're not successful until you've fulfilled your purpose.

Instead of chasing false success, I chose to add value to others by informing them, educating them, and empowering them with resources that can positively impact their lives, and I strive to be an example to other entrepreneurs that they can follow to create a better life for themselves, their families, and the community by operating with integrity and purpose.

Once you determine what your passion, purpose, and plan for life is, you have to know how you're going to achieve them. This part of the process is where many people become distracted. You have to identify what skills, talents, and abilities you possess that you can use on your journey. Many people aren't able to recognize God's favor on their lives because they have been taught that your achievements are a result of how much they know. But when God's favor and inspiration is on you, you achieve based on who you are, not what you know.

I realized that my ability to interact with people, my skill of making something out of nothing (just like I did with that old U-Haul truck), and my talents in creating, selling, and managing would be enough for me to achieve true success because I trusted God for it.

There's a popular saying that "God doesn't call the equipped, He equips those whom He calls." Don't wait to have the resources, skills, or talents you think you need to succeed. God will provide them as you follow Him.

God gives all of us unique skills, talents, and abilities, even if we don't always recognize them for what they are. Many of us negate these natural attributes as signs of what our passion, purpose, and plan really is because they may come to us easily. That's kind of the point. They're gifts. Whatever you're doing in life should align with your attributes. If you're good with your hands, or with people, that's a gift. Learn to recognize what skills God has equipped you with and allow them to lead you to your passion.

I knew that if I were going to experience true success, I had to be doing something for the rest of my life that aligned with what I did well and enjoyed doing. It pleases God when we're doing something with what He has given us.

Another component of seizing the opportunity of true success is identifying the community you're going to serve. Ask yourself these questions to start. There may be others, but begin with these:

- What community is in need of your skill set, your unique abilities, and your talents?
- What problem can you solve for this community?
- What products or services are lacking within this community?
- How can you improve the products and services that already exist in the community?
- Who can you collaborate with to serve this community?

The community I've determined to serve is entrepreneurs. Small business owners have a unique set of issues. Unfortunately, many entrepreneurs do not have access to the resources, support, and information that could aid their success. As a result, they never fully reach their potential, and they have to compete against large corporations that have all the things that I mentioned. The failure rate for small business owners is staggering. If we can get more small business owners to realize what true success is, make them aware of their full potential, and provide them with the resources they need, we all will benefit.

Finally, the last step of practicing true success is the way you're going to serve this community.

- Will it be through ministry?
- Will you start a business in the community?
- Is there an existing company in the community that embodies the same objective as you that could use your expertise?
- Are you able to use your skills, abilities, and talents in a nonprofit, organization, or partnership that is committed to impacting the community?

Too many people commit to a career at a company because "it's hiring." We must begin to choose careers that reflect or serve purpose, not only for a paycheck. Entrepreneurs can serve the community through several different avenues because they normally have a passion for many things.

I personally have several ways I serve the community, I'm an agency owner, a licensed funeral director, and embalmer, speaker, trainer, and coach.

This book is also another stream of adding value to others. Your value, how you contribute to your community, may be different. It's not a competition. It's a process. In I Corinthians 12:12, Paul writes, "For just as the body is one and has many members, and all the members of the body, though many, are one body, so it is with Christ." Not everyone in the body or community is a "hand," "head," or "foot." Everyone is a part of the body of believers and has their own purpose. What I have to offer may not be what you have to offer. My offerings are not "better" or "worse" any more than it's better or worse to be a hand or a foot. We're all part of a larger, greater whole.

Success is an ongoing process. Achieving smaller goals of the big picture is practicing true success. As you can see, most of us are practicing true success in our own ways. Some of us educate, cook, or are drivers, barbers, service providers, factory workers, nurses, and homemakers. Although you might not get an award for what you do or become rich and famous, you're doing what you're called to do. Whatever you do, do it in excellence.

9

MOMENTUM OF TRUE SUCCESS

As you get closer to success first you're sure you're dying, that it's all over, that you've permanently failed. Then something happens and suddenly you feel reborn.

~Steven D. Compton

Maintaining momentum with my life, my business, and my day-to-day tasks is the biggest challenge I've experienced while practicing success. What do I mean by momentum? It is the strength or force that something has when it is moving. As long as that thing is moving, it has momentum. Momentum is necessary for achieving true success. You have to keep moving to become and stay successful.

You'd think it would be easy to keep moving once you're rolling, but it's not. Think about it like this: success is like a snowball. You start off with smaller successes, like a small snowball. The more you push, the larger it becomes. The bigger it gets, the harder it is to push. That force that is working against the snowball and your success is called "friction."

Friction is the resistance or object that is working against something or someone in motion. If you were rolling a huge snowball on a sheet of ice, it would roll easily. But if you're pushing it through five inches of fresh, powdered snow or uphill, it's harder. It's the same snowball, but a different level of effort is required to maintain momentum. Why? Because of friction. In the world of snowballs, the ground is the thing that creates friction. In life, the friction we encounter can be a lack of spirituality, haters, emotions, physicality, education, skills, time, money, and resources.

Depending on how much friction you have, it can be harder and take longer to maintain momentum or overcome the friction. Think about a time when you were hired to do your dream job. If everything went smoothly, you didn't have any friction, so it was easy to maintain momentum. It was easy! Now imagine that same event but with everything going wrong. Maybe your supervisor was always on your back, the company you worked for decided to lay off its employees, your car broke down, or your employer raised the quota 100 percent. Those things are friction. They make it harder to maintain momentum.

The same thing can happen with an entrepreneur. You might get your loan all lined up and have no problems with the bank. Your grand opening is huge, and lots of people spend lots of money. There is no friction. Or you can have a lot of friction. Your loan is denied, your product shipment for your grand opening is delayed, or it rains on the one day you have an outside event. You get sick. Your employees get sick and leave you alone to run the store. Friction slows down your momentum. If you don't understand what's happening, it's easy to get discouraged and quit.

The problem with most people in general is that they don't have enough experience with the process to recognize how momentum and friction work.

There's a point between starting off as a solo entrepreneur to having an operation that is running like a well-oiled machine that momentum starts to slow and progress becomes the most difficult, which stops many people. This is the point at which we all want to quit. There's just too much friction. It feels like you're pushing that snowball or business uphill, even if you're on flat ground. Not only are you trying to grow, you're trying to gain momentum, while at the same time battling the forces of gravity and friction. You know if you stop pushing at any time, the snowball will not grow, and it won't move forward, either. That's OK for short periods of time. We all need to rest. But if it goes on too long, it's incredibly difficult to build up momentum again.

If you understand how friction works, how to reduce it, and how to find the sweet spot, or you get some help pushing that snowball along, that snowball, or your business, will get bigger and bigger. Eventually, they'll both begin gaining momentum on their own and start rolling along with less effort. All of a sudden, you'll have so much momentum that you won't have to push it anymore because the momentum is overcoming the amount of friction it had before. The size, weight, and momentum will have overcome the obstacles of gravity and friction. That amount of momentum will then become an avalanche of true success, plowing over every sign of failure, defeat, and fear.

The beauty of having momentum is it makes it much easier to endure challenges and obstacles.

One of the most expensive lessons I've had was when I had to sell the assets (book of business) of my agency. I had started my insurance agency in 2005. I signed a contract to represent one of the largest insurance companies in the country. After two years as a commission-only sales rep for my mentor, I was finally on my own. Business was good because I had a niche that was really paying off for my business.

I created a circle of influence of mortgage brokers that referred clients who needed property insurance for homes they were purchasing or refinancing. Two days a week, I would canvas the streets of metro Atlanta, looking for mortgage brokers who wanted to partner together to provide better customer experiences for their clients. Over time, I developed relationships with dozens of mortgage brokers. This target market yielded a great return for my business. I had a great deal of momentum.

I was receiving referrals for clients who needed property insurance left and right. Business was good, at least until the 2008 recession and the collapse of the housing market. Since my client base was primarily made up of homeowners and real estate investors, after the real estate bubble burst, my business began to fail. That is when I realized, along with millions of other small business owners, that I did not have enough momentum to withstand the recession.

Not only did the referrals stop, but my existing clients were dropping like flies. I remember receiving hundreds of returned insurance documents from clients because their homes were considered vacant. My clients were walking away from their homes because they either lost their jobs or the adjustable mortgage rates increased. My client base was shrinking. Consequently, my income was shrinking. I wanted out. I decided to sell the assets of my agency in 2010. Because I was afraid and concerned, I took the first offer someone made. It was a fraction of what I should have gotten.

It was a bad experience, but I learned an important lesson. Diversify your client base, and never rely on one target market to be the source to grow your business. Have a mix of clientele from various sectors, industries, or classes. Don't put all your eggs in one basket. Another lesson I learned from this situation is to always have a price for your business. Don't wait until you're panicked, worried, or strapped for cash to decide on a price. Those things will cloud your common sense and good judgement. Know what your business is worth before you need to know it.

Have a business plan, including an exit strategy and a succession strategy. Having a business plan is vital for your business to grow, but what is your plan if it stops growing or you decide to go in a different direction? You should have a succession plan from day one, even if you don't believe you'll ever need it. Consider it insurance that will protect you when the unexpected happens.

So, what's your business worth today? If someone is better prepared to buy you out than you are to sell your business, you will always get less money than you expected, and you will regret it for a long, long time. Have a succession package ready at all times.

It's a funny thing about life. We never learn everything we need to know in just one lesson, no matter how painful that lesson. I've had more painful and expensive lessons than I can count.

Another memorable and expensive lesson I had took place after I sold the assets of my first insurance agency. The 2008 recession had beaten me up pretty badly. I was, by no means, giving up on entrepreneurship. But I learned I had to diversify in business.

I spent the next few weeks after selling my business looking for an insurance carrier whom I could represent without the heavy concentration on homeowner's insurance, the very thing that hurt my business in 2008 and 2009. I finally found a company that specialized in various products for a niche market. This insurance carrier specialized in financial products for educators. The business model was much different than what I was accustomed to. In order to be successful with this carrier, it would take much longer and require hundreds of "kitchen table" presentations. My dream of owning a large, self-sustaining insurance agency was not possible there. But it would give me the necessary time I needed to diversify, seize various opportunities, and expand outside the one industry. When we feel this confident about something is usually when we're getting ready to learn another expensive lesson. And I was definitely headed down the path to getting schooled yet again.

This is when I made one of the biggest mistakes I've made as an entrepreneur. Like many startup entrepreneurs, I chose to start a business strictly on the notation that it makes money. I was not led by my passion, purpose, or plan. I decided that I wanted to get in the tax preparation business, not because I was passionate about taxes, but because I was focused on making money. Of course, my mind was on money; I'd just lost a lot of it and wanted to recoup my losses. I broke my own rule of passion, plan, and purpose to choose a career path that wasn't part of my vision.

I researched several tax preparation franchises and was impressed by many of them. But the franchise fees were too high. Then I came across a small, family-owned tax preparation franchise. They had expanded in the Atlanta area a couple years prior to my inquiry. It seemed to be a perfect fit. The franchise fee was a reasonable, and the business model was attractive. I still was reluctant to pay the franchise fee because I was afraid that this might not be the business for me. Although I was intrigued by the income potential, I was not passionately motivated. As a result, fear was present. I began focusing on every alternative result.

The experts tell us that one of the four major decisions we should never make while we're grieving or after suffering a huge loss is to sell our house, get rid of mementos, move, or change jobs. I was just coming off a major loss of money and a business sale where I didn't get what I should have for selling.

But I had to make a decision, or I thought I did. I had a plan. This franchise opportunity gave franchisees three franchise agreements for the price of one. Most franchises want a fee for each location. I just wasn't ready to part with $10,000 for the franchise fee. So I had to think of a way to get in this business.

I contacted a franchisee in the Atlanta area, and I asked if she had any plans for opening up the other two franchise locations available to her. This particular franchisee did not have the desire to run multiple locations. So I gave her an offer to do a twelve-month operating agreement with an option to purchase one of her locations. It worked out for both of us. She got an extra couple thousand dollars for a location she was never going to open. And I got in the franchise for a fraction of the franchise fee. So far, so good.

I was now in the tax preparation business. The first step was to go through the franchise's training program. I had to travel to the small town of Russellville, Arkansas, for the four-day training at the home office. This family had mastered the income tax prep business and created a system that they decided to package and sell as a franchise. They didn't have fancy signage, office furniture, and decor like the big-box income tax franchises. But they had a track record of doing *big* numbers, and they could teach others how to do the same.

I learned a system there that I still use in all my businesses today. This company's file processing system was awesome. They had processes that eliminated errors and mistakes in the processing of clients' income taxes. Just like their office, their tax preparation system was not fancy, automated, or complicated, but it was flawless. At any given moment, you would know the status of a client's account based on where the physical file was in the processing room. It was an assembly line for client files. It reminded me of a McDonald's restaurant. This was how this small family tax office was able to generate more tax returns than many of the other big-box tax franchises in the area. Yes, they had good staff. Yes, they had good marketing programs. But the processing system was gold. The tax preparers knew when tax season came; all they had to do was prepare taxes and not deal with the back-end issues of processing errors. It was a machine.

Then I had to find an office. I spent several thousand dollars building a tiny office on the west side of Atlanta. Next, I built a staff of three good preparers. I was ready for the tax season.

I hated it! I can't really explain what the feeling was. But I did not have the passion for it. I quickly learned that this was not God's plan for me. Once again, I was being led by visions and dreams of false success.

Tax preparation is not much different than the insurance business, so I thought. And truthfully, it's not that much different. But it is a different plan. And most importantly, it was not in my plan. Business was slow, and I was losing money quickly. I knew that this business would take a few years to get it where I wanted it to be. I just didn't like it. I decided one tax season was enough for me. It was one of the most expensive business lessons I've ever learned; I lost around $30,000. The best thing about that whole experience was learning the tax service processing from the franchisee. I still use it today when I train and coach other business owners. I tell them that this one technique cost me $30,000. So the fee for my entire coaching program is a drop in the bucket of what I've spent on this entrepreneurial journey.

Whether you're a new entrepreneur or a seasoned one, you'll notice that I've told you as much about my failures as I have about my successes, maybe more. A lot of business owners prefer not to think about their failures or the times they made poor or just outright bad decisions. I don't know many people who enjoy sharing the times they failed, looked foolish, made bad decisions, or outright screwed things up. It's not fun being that vulnerable or looking that silly or stupid in front of other people, especially people who will use our weaknesses and failures against us.

So, why do it? Well, have you ever watched a baby learning to walk? The parents are there cheering him/her on, even when that baby falls, trips, or gives up and goes back to crawling. The parents focus on the steps the baby does take, not on all the failures. They know their child is learning to walk, and they're excited about it. The baby who gets a lot of encouragement, hugs, cheers, and laughter during the process will learn faster than one who is ignored or criticized during the learning process. I like to think of God the Father as that proud parent who is watching me learning to "walk" and who is cheering me on, even through my failures and the times I fall. He knows I'm learning, and He's excited for me.

When I share my failures with other entrepreneurs, I can see that they have experienced failures, too, and that they are encouraged by my words. I'm not trying to show them up. I'm encouraging them and letting them know we *all* fail, but that getting up, dusting ourselves off, and learning from the experience is what makes us winners, and successful.

You might not believe it, but failure is where you'll find your biggest successes. If you don't believe it, think about this man. He started and failed in business at age twenty-one. He decided to go into politics but was defeated in a legislative race at age twenty-two. He went back to giving business a shot, but failed again at age twenty-four. It wasn't just business and politics he suffered in. He had to overcome the death of his fiancée when he only twenty-six. The grief and losses took their toll on him, and at age twenty-seven, he had a nervous breakdown. He came back, stronger, more focused, and determined to give politics another go, but he lost a congressional race at thirty-four. Then he lost a senatorial race at age forty-five. He kept on going in politics, even when he failed to become vice president at age forty-seven. He lost another senatorial race at forty-nine but didn't give up. Then, at age fifty-two, he was elected president of the United States. This man was Abraham Lincoln. He refused to let his failures define him. He repeatedly fought against significant odds to achieve greatness.

If you look at every character in the Bible, both in the Old and New Testament, you'll see that there are more details about the failures of the men and women of God than there are successes. And when there are successes, they inevitably come as results of failure. No one ever steps up to be a servant of God without experiencing multiple failures, testing, and challenges.

Moses wandered in the desert for forty years, tending sheep and goats after having been a prince in an Egyptian family. God called him to serve, and he spent another forty years wandering in the desert while the people he was trying to help criticized, cursed, and attacked him for every God-led decision he made. Then he disobeyed God and ended up never entering the land of "milk and honey" himself.

1. **Don't make failure personal.** Failure is not about who you are, it's about something that happened to you. Remember how often, how publicly, and how major Abraham Lincoln's failures were? Yet he persisted, never giving up, never being shamed or humiliated into quitting for good. I often wonder how his faith in God sustained him. Lincoln frequently referred to God and had a deep knowledge of the Bible, often quoting from it. He grew up in a highly religious Baptist family, and while historians believe he strayed from his faith for a while, he obviously believed in God, prayed, and believed that God was intervening in the affairs of the United States of America. Failure is necessary if you are to succeed. Henry Ford, the most famous name in automobile manufacturing, wasn't always a success. His first two automobile companies failed. Albert Einstein's parents were convinced he was mentally retarded. He didn't speak until he turned four and didn't read until he was seven; his teachers told him he would "never amount to anything." He proved them wrong. Einstein was regarded as the most important scientist of the twentieth century. He was awarded the 1921 Nobel Prize for Physics.

    Bill Gates, founder of Microsoft, and Steve Jobs, founder of Apple, both dropped out of college. Jobs was even homeless in his twenties, collecting cans for money and eating at a Buddhist soup kitchen once a week. Jim Carrey, Suze Orman (financial wizard and Oprah's number one financial advisor), Halle Berry, David Letterman, and hundreds of other celebrities were all once homeless. They didn't let that "failure" stop them from moving forward, which is why we know their names as some of the most famous celebrities of the last fifty years.

    It's almost impossible for anyone reading this book to have never seen a Walt Disney movie or cartoon. He's that famous. Yet

Disney started his first business from his home garage. His very first cartoon production went bankrupt, and for years, he fought people's perception of him as being "strange," and a loser and untalented. People laughed at his idea of a talking, singing mouse; yet who today doesn't know who Mickey Mouse is?

Oprah Winfrey was fired from her television reporting job. Her producer told her she was a bad reporter and that she wasn't suited for television. I think she definitely proved everyone wrong on that count. I can go on and on. You'd be surprised how many famous people you know were failures and who were turned down and put down throughout their lives and careers. Google "famous failures," and you'll see what I mean.

2. **Review, adapt, and learn from failure.** Failure happens. Don't run from it when it does. Sit down and objectively examine what happened and why. Every police and fire department and medical team in the country does this after a mission, fire, or surgery so they can look at what went wrong and what went right. It's called a "debriefing," and teams do it so they can learn from both their successes and their failures.

3. **Win or lose, but don't dwell on the outcome for longer than twenty-four hours.** Good coaches understand the need for their players to grieve their losses. They know that all of us need time to wallow in our pity or revel in our joy, but only for so long. Coaches, managers, and leaders in all walks of life follow Don Shula's policy regarding wins and losses (Shula is the winningest coach in the NFL, holding the record for most career wins, including two Super Bowl victories).

Shula had a "twenty-four-hour rule," which was his policy of looking forward instead of dwelling on the past. Players, staff, and those working with the team, himself included, were allowed to celebrate a victory or brood over a defeat for only twenty-four hours. During those hours, they were encouraged to feel their emotions of success or failure as deeply as they could. Then, the next day, it was time to put that win or that loss behind them and focus on preparing for their next challenge. Shula believed in keeping both wins and losses in perspective and focusing on the future, not the past.

4. **Give up the need for other people's approval.** The only approval you should be seeking should be God's. Many of us don't fear failure unless we know others will see us fail and judge us. When you are working on something in private and you know no one is going to see you make a mistake, you don't obsess about failing much. Why? Our fear of failure is mostly rooted in our fear of being judged and losing others' respect and esteem. We want people to think we're capable, strong, smart, and talented. No one wants to look weak or look like a failure or loser in front of others. It's why we get so angry when someone "disses" us or plays a joke on us that makes us look silly. The anger we feel at those times is really the fear of looking foolish and losing people's respect and approval. When you learn to stop needing other people's approval is, oddly enough, when they start giving you all their support and approval! Learn to depend on your own approval, that of God's, and that of people who love you and support you unconditionally.

5. **Recognize and admit failure as soon as possible.** The most important part of failing is recognizing it for what it is: a failure. Too many of us try to "spin" our failures, downplay them, or even deny something was a failure. We hang on, hoping that we'll be able to pull them off, even after those around us know they're dead.

   The fastest way to learn from and move on from failure of any size is to recognize it was a failure, admit it was a failure, and then move on. Once you have conceded something was a failure, you are free to step away from it and look at it to see what went wrong, what went right, what you could have done differently or better, and how you can try again, with a better plan.

Failure is only deadly if you don't get back up and try again.

10

TRUE SUCCESS

True success is the pursuit of your passion, purpose, and plan.

~Steve D. Compton

There really isn't a "secret to success." The path is plain to anyone who wants to look for it. The problem is not that there is some big secret to becoming a success. It's that people don't want to do what they need to do to become successful. Everyone wants a magic pill or quick fix. No one wants to work for success. And if I have a "secret," it's that the secret to succeeding isn't really a secret at all. It's about putting God and others before yourself. It's about genuinely caring about your faith, your God, your family, and your community, and utilizing the skills, talents, and purpose God gave you. If you want to know how to succeed, here's my list. I guarantee, if you follow it, you too will succeed!

PLEASE GOD

The Bible tells us that there's only *one* way to please God: by having faith. God (in His word, the Bible) says all that it is necessary for us to please Him and to seek Him by faith, walk in the Spirit and not in the flesh, and walk worthy of our calling in obedience and submission to His will. We don't have to do anything, or pile up good works, or be perfect. We just have to have faith and believe and trust in God. It's harder than it sounds. And it requires spending time getting to know Him through studying the Bible. I have spent thousands of hours learning all I know about contracts, insurance, and business because it's my life. It doesn't make sense not to spend at least that much time studying, getting to know my creator, and being totally responsible for where I am today! Learn how to please God, then please Him by developing your faith.

FOLLOWING AND TRUSTING GOD

Some people laugh. Some people roll their eyes. Some bite their tongue and some just look confused when I tell them I succeed because I follow and trust God. I can't explain it to you if you aren't a believer who knows God, but let me just say the Bible is my operations manual, and God is the one who designed, built, and knows me inside out.

When I "follow and trust God," all I'm doing is adhering to the instructions, guidance, and operations manual of the being who knows me better than I know myself. Who wouldn't follow a plan for their lives by their creator if they understood that doing so would bring them all the success they could handle and then some?

TREATING YOUR CUSTOMERS WITH RESPECT

The first time I read this verse in Hebrews 13:2, I got chills. I still do every time I read it. If you don't, you're not thinking about it. It goes:

> *"Do not neglect to show hospitality to strangers, for thereby some have entertained angels unawares."*

Think about it. What if that stranger you just honked at, that person you bumped into and didn't stop to apologize, or that elderly woman on the bus you pretended not to see so you wouldn't have to give up your seat, was an angel in disguise? What if you conducted your business as though you believed everyone you came into contact with was an angel in disguise? How would your life (and theirs) be different? If the Bible says it, at some point, it's going to be true. Someone you interact with is going to be a real, honest-to-goodness angel from God. How would you feel if that encounter was a negative one?

I guarantee if you treat your customers, your potential customers, and total strangers with kindness, humbleness, and an attitude of servitude and love, you will always be a success.

SELF-DISCIPLINE

If you can't get out of bed, get to your job on time, or do the things you need to do to succeed, you won't succeed. Self-discipline isn't about "feeling motivated" and then doing something. Self-discipline is about doing something when you don't feel motivated at all!

Self-discipline is a very, very difficult thing to develop as an adult, but it's not impossible. If you're young enough, the military will teach you self-discipline quickly. If you're lucky enough to have parents, coaches, and teachers who care about you, they can also teach you self-discipline. If you're all alone, you're going to have to teach yourself.

Self-discipline is the ability to control your feelings and overcome your weaknesses, even if you don't *feel* like doing so. It's the ability to pursue what you think is right or desirable, despite temptations to abandon your efforts. More than anything, self-discipline is the ability to give up instant and immediate gratification and pleasure in favor of some greater gain or more satisfying results, even if this requires effort and time. The Olympic athlete who gives up time with his friends to go to practice every day is one example. The entrepreneur who stays home to work on his business rather than go out to dinner or partying with friends is another.

Self-discipline is the ability to see and work toward your future when other people, things, sleep, hobbies, and issues are doing all they can to distract you from your goal. We all struggle with this. Even Christ's disciples struggled, and they equated their struggle with running a race. In Philippians 3:14, Paul tells his readers, *"I press on toward the goal to win the prize for which God has called me heavenward in Christ Jesus."* Paul kept his eyes focused on the ultimate prize.

That doesn't mean being self-disciplined is a punishment or that you have to live a restricted lifestyle. Self-discipline isn't about punishing yourself. It's about having the inner strength and staying power you need to achieve your goals. It's about having the mental and emotional strength to choose what you want rather than let your emotions, temptations, or distractions of the moment steer you in a different direction. A self-disciplined person asks him- or herself: "Will doing this instead of what I am doing now bring me closer to my goals or take me away from them?" If having dinner with a colleague rather than working on your business plan will honestly bring you closer to your goals of your own business, then have dinner with them. If it will simply be fun and a distraction, then acknowledge you're deciding to delay your goals to have fun. It's a choice. You don't *have* to do anything. You choose to.

TIME MANAGEMENT

We all have twenty-four hours in a day, no more, no less. Even Moses and Noah (who spent more than one hundred years in building the Ark) had twenty-four hours in their days. Here's my secret to managing my time: I don't manage my time; I manage my attention. I choose what and whom to focus on because "it's what you focus on that gets done." If you don't believe that, ask yourself how many brush fires you put out in a day. Brush fires get our attention (and by brush fires, I mean urgent things that come up during the day that don't really advance you toward your goals but that demand your attention because they're so loud and immediate).

For instance, if I want to ensure something gets done, I put it on a to-do list. I also make an appointment with myself to do it at a specific time. If I know I have to do reports and paperwork, I put it in my calendar to sit down at a specific time and do it, just like I'd schedule time with a client or a date. A study by Heidi Grant Halvorson, a Columbia University professor, shows that "when you decide in advance when and where you will take specific actions to reach your goal can double or triple your chances for success."

Imagine! All you have to do is (1) write down your goals, (2) schedule the things you have to do to accomplish them, and (3) follow through.

HONESTY

No one wants to do business or even be in a relationship with someone who isn't honest or trustworthy. One of the big issues with drug dealers has to do with trust. They don't trust one another, and both buyers, sellers, and customers spend more time worrying about getting ripped off, mugged, or shot and killed than they do about making money.

Honesty is more than telling the truth. It's about being authentic and owning up to mistakes when you make them. It's about not overpolishing the apple, meaning making people think you're better, more experienced, or in better shape than you really are. I'm not saying spill all your dirty laundry to the world, but if you're struggling with something, let your employees know what's appropriate for them to know. You don't claim to be an expert in something you're not. You don't put the "everything is coming up roses" spin on things if there are some aspects to the business you're struggling with. You're humble and honest, and you don't try to make people think you're something you're not or that you're doing better than you truly are.

INTEGRITY

Integrity is the quality of being honest and having strong moral principles and moral uprightness. Even if you can't explain it, most of us know what it is. When we have and demonstrate integrity, we draw people to us. People do business with people they like and trust. People who do the right thing, even when it's the hardest thing, show integrity.

Integrity is doing what we know to be the honest, right, moral, or ethical thing to do, even when no one is looking. It's a character trait. You have it or you don't. Integrity is strict adherence to a moral code. You don't have to be a Christian to have integrity. People of all faiths and beliefs follow moral codes.

Integrity is something that coworkers, customers, and the public will spot, even if you think you're hiding nonethical behavior. People with integrity recognize others with it.

FAITH

Faith is what you believe in. You may or may not be a Christian. I'm not here to tell you what to believe in, although I'm sharing my own faith. But you must have faith in something greater than yourself. You must believe there is a plan for your life, a reason for living, and a force that is bigger, more intelligent, and loving than you are. If your faith is in your business, your integrity, your values, so be it. But know what it is you believe in. Be able to articulate it.

ADDING VALUE TO OTHERS

When is the last time you walked away from a conversation with someone that made you feel truly heard? It's rare for most of us to talk to someone and feel like that person really understood us, let alone valued us for what we had to say. When we listen to family, customers, strangers, or coworkers, the greatest value we can add to them, their lives, or their day is to listen to them in a way that makes them feel heard. Yes, it's a skill most of us have to develop, but it's possible. When people walk away feeling heard, they also feel like they know you better because they feel like you understand them!

Listening is not a passive skill. It takes work. Humans think at a rate of about five hundred words per minute, but most people speak at a rate of only one hundred fifty words per minute. Instead of using that gap to think about what's being said, most of us use that extra time to think about other things and then become distracted. People notice that, even if you think they don't. Instead of thinking about *your other things*, think about questions you can ask to get the speaker to share even more with you.

If you're not a good listener, start learning how to improve. Read books and articles, practice on your friends and colleagues, or just start noticing the people who listen to you most effectively and ask them their secrets.

LEAVING A LEGACY FOR YOUR FAMILY AND COMMUNITY

Among all the people I've talked to in my life, I've never met one who came into this world holding physical money or property or one that left this world taking physical or financial wealth with them. Property, money, and things don't last, but a legacy will. A legacy is something that a person leaves behind to be remembered by. What kind of legacy are you leaving for your family? Have you taught your children the skills, morals, and values they'll need to carry on your legacy of honesty, humbleness, faith, and integrity? Are you leaving behind a legacy of a family that helps others, volunteers, or is a benefit and an asset to its community?

What kind of legacy are you leaving your community? This may be what kind of company you built. Is it one that will continue to honor your work, ethics, and standards for business and customer service? You may leave a legacy of giving to charitable causes or doing projects for your community that enhances and improves the lives of those in it. Do something so that who and what you are and what you stand for doesn't disappear when you're gone.

PURSUING YOUR PASSION, PURPOSE, AND PLAN

I can't emphasize enough how important it is to follow your passion, purpose, and plan. I mentioned earlier how miserable I was in a good business that was one I really cared little about. It can be the best opportunity in the world, but if your heart, passion, and purpose isn't in it, you won't be there for long, either.

It may take a while for you to discover what really makes you wake up and want to run to your office in the morning, but take your time learning what that is. Chances are, you'll be doing whatever it is you do for a long time. Make sure it's right. If, like I did, you get into a situation and discover it's not for you, get out. You're just wasting time.

How do you find your passion, purpose, and plan? You try things. You talk to people. You read. You pray. You look. You'll have to get your feet wet and your hands dirty, as they say. That means you have to actually do it, not just think about it. Reality is different than vision.

CREATING OPPORTUNITIES FOR OTHERS

The best way to get ahead is to help others get what they want. The person who said it first, that I know of, is Zig Zigler. He said, "You will *get* all you *want* in life, if you *help* enough other people *get what they want.*" I have found this to be very true.

The main reason people don't do this is they think there's "not enough to go around." They have a scarcity mentality. They think if someone else gets something, they won't get theirs. They try too hard to hang onto all they've got, no matter what it is, and to keep others from getting what they want.

There's an old story about a dog in a manger, some hay, and some cows. The dog was sleeping on a huge pile of hay in a manger when the cattle of the field came into the barn. They started nibbling at the hay, but the dog jumped up and barked at them, scaring them away. The cows said, "Why do you care? You can't possibly sleep on all this hay. Share with us." The dog snarled and said, "No, this is my hay." The cows went away, understanding that at some point, the dog would leave, and then the hay would be theirs. The moral of the story is, "People often begrudge others what they cannot enjoy themselves." Don't do this. If you have something, share it. If you know of a connection that would help someone, introduce them. Be generous, even when you worry about your own opportunities. I've often seen someone help someone else, and that person goes on to become a success and able to return the favor. You never know who is going to benefit and remember you.

When you help others and create opportunities for them, that comes back to you. It may take days, months, or years, but helping others is never a loss. If someone doesn't pay you back directly, they may help others down the road.

I once heard a story; I don't know if it's true or not, but it goes something like this: a very wealthy woman's car broke down outside of town. Her money was no good with no one to call. She was beginning to freeze in the cold weather when a young man happened along. He fixed her car, and when she tried to pay him, he refused. "Pay it forward," he told her. "Help someone else down the road when you can." She thanked him and drove on into town. She stopped for a cup of hot coffee and pie at a local diner. The waitress who waited on her was friendly, pretty, and very pregnant. The woman thought about what the young man said about paying it forward, and before she left, she gave the young woman a $500 tip, thinking that the waitress would need the extra money for the new baby. The woman also left a note on the napkin, "Someone helped me tonight and told me pay it forward. So I am."

That night, when the waitress got home, she kissed her husband and asked, "How was your day?"

He shrugged. "OK. I helped a woman whose car broke down outside of town. She offered to pay me, and I know we need the money, but I refused. I told her to pay it forward."

The young woman froze, then reached into her pocket and handed her husband the money and the note. "She did."

We never know who we're going to bless or how they're going to bless us, but I guarantee that if you are generous, your blessing will be packed into and overflow your life.

BLESSING OTHERS

I've met people along the way who I decided would be better off locked away from people for life. There was no way I was going to have anything to do with them, let alone bless them! But God has a way of changing your mind if you let Him. He blesses the good and the bad. The secret is, you don't treat people based on who they are. You treat them based on who you are and on what your character is. If you allow people to make you angry, mean, and vindictive because they are unpleasant or a jerk, then you're letting others define who you are.

You become, like Christ said, "a man driven to and fro by the wind," if you only treat people the way they treat you. If you bless some people and not others, you're not really showing people who you are and what your character is. People will say, "If you're nice to him, he's OK, but if you're not nice, he hates on you." They will pretend to be nice to play you.

If you're nice to everyone, bless everyone, and behave like God— treating everyone, good or bad, with kindness and respect—you will get respect.

RECOGNITION FROM YOUR PEERS AND COLLEAGUES

It's important to get recognition from your peers and colleagues, but not to change who you are to get it. I mean it's nice to have their support, respect, and encouragement, but not at the expense of who you are or what your faith is. The only person you should really seek approval and recognition from is Jesus Christ and God the Father. That's the recognition you should value most.

The respect of men (and that includes women) makes us feel good, but the respect and recognition of God and His approval is what makes each of us the kind of person people respect, too.

Be honest, authentic, loving, generous, helpful, and kind to others, and the recognition will follow.

PROVING "THEM" WRONG

I think one of the strongest motivators for any of us is to prove our naysayers and critics wrong. If they say we "can't" do something, we will double our efforts to prove them wrong. There's just something satisfying about being right, especially when our being right means someone else has to reconsider their evaluation of us.

I don't have a gift of reading people's minds, but I can guess, based on life experience, that many of the successful people in industry today were as motivated as I was by people who told me I couldn't do something. If you can't find any other motivator, that's as good as any. Eventually you'll want to do things for yourself, but I support any legal method to light that spark!

BEATING THE ODDS

When people talk about "beating the odds," they're talking about the chances someone has of overcoming obstacles in their lives. The more obstacles, the greater the likelihood that person will give up. We say they couldn't beat the odds. The problem with that kind of thinking is that, one, it's negative, and two, it leaves out the powers of God, faith, and passion. A person with drive, passion, something to prove, and a faith in God can pretty much overcome any odds.

Go back to the Bible and look at David, a twelve-year-old shepherd boy who killed Goliath, a nine-foot-tall, professionally trained giant, with a sling and a rock. What are the odds of that happening? Not only that, David was prepared to kill Goliath's bigger brothers! What I find most fascinating about the story of David and Goliath was that David didn't just rush blindly into the battle. He beat the odds because he did two things:

He used what he knew and the skills he had confidence in. He wasn't a soldier and never fought in battle, but he did know how to use a rock and sling. According to the Bible, he *had* killed bears and lions with his sling. He was a master at what he knew, and he wasn't going to let others sway him from his practiced skills. I knew what I was good at. When those sales managers told me that I couldn't do the job because I didn't have their skills, tools, and background (college), they were doing the same thing the soldiers did to David. They tried to tell him he would fail because he wasn't doing things their way. David proved them wrong, and I proved the sales managers wrong. Just because you don't have the advantages, tools, skills, education, and background that someone else has doesn't mean you can't succeed. David succeeded where the best, strongest, and most experienced soldiers had failed. And he did it with a rock and a sling.

He admitted to himself and others what he was weak at, and he refused to let others tell him how to do things. Read the story again. Once David said he wanted to kill Goliath, the soldiers tried to have him do it their way. They dressed him up in their armor, gave him a sword and the tools of their trade, and tried to send him off to do battle like they would have, had they had the courage to fight. But David immediately recognized that the armor, sword, and helmet would slow him down and possibly get him killed. He had no problem admitting what he was weak at, which was being a soldier. So he refused their help, advice, and equipment and *did it his way*, with rocks and a sling. He knew his weakness, but he knew his strengths, too, and he used them both.

OVERCOMING OBSTACLES
People think that once you've "made it" and you're a success, or you reach the top in your field, there are no more obstacles. I'll let you in on a secret. There are more obstacles. I hate to be the one to break it to you, but we never, ever stop encountering roadblocks while we're alive and on this planet. The Devil will see to that. The more you practice success, the more the Devil will try to derail you.

The kinds of obstacles you'll encounter when you're successful will be different than what you face when you're struggling to make a living or start a business. You'll encounter jealousy or people who think you cheated your way to the top, just "got lucky," or knew someone who let you bypass the hard work. You've just got to remember that obstacles of any kind—physical, mental, emotional, or spiritual—are just part of being alive. Don't take them personally, even if they feel very personal. Remember that it's the Devil trying to take you down, and thank God for His help and protection.

DEFEATING THE DEVIL IN AREAS WHERE YOU ARE ATTACKED

Like I said, the Devil is always going to attack you, often in subtle ways that feel like personal betrayal rather than demonic attack. The Devil isn't some red-horned monster. The Bible tells us he appears as an "angel of light" and wisdom. What appears to be a good thing can be a bad thing. You can be tempted to do things that look or feel good but aren't.

We don't fight people. Ephesians 6:12 says, "For our struggle is not against flesh and blood, but against the rulers, against the authorities, against the powers of this dark world and against the spiritual forces of evil in the heavenly realms." Learn to conduct spiritual warfare, pray, and test the spirits of good and evil.

Remember, the Devil attacked Jesus Himself, so no one is safe from his assaults.

Here are some things to keep in mind about the Devil's attacks. He will attack you when:

You have just had an uplifting or positive spiritual experience. You may have attended a great retreat, Bible study, or sermon. You are feeling powerful and connected to God. So, remember, after a great spiritual experience, expect and prepare for an attack.

You've started a new spiritual endeavor. Maybe you just found a new place of worship, recommitted your faith, or you're trying to. Maybe you joined a new Bible study or started a new ministry. Expect an attack. The Devil doesn't want us enjoying life or helping others, and he will do all he can to derail you when you're most vulnerable, which is at the beginning of a new spiritual endeavor.

You're alone. If you're used to being around friends, family, church members, or others who encourage and support you, be aware, the Devil will attack when you're alone. You may be tempted to watch movies you shouldn't be watching or to talk to people who may not be the best people to talk to. You may have thoughts or feelings that lead you down a dark path. When you're alone, you're more likely to feel lonely, depressed, or discouraged. You're more likely to listen to negative self-talk. The Devil attacked Jesus when he went into the wilderness alone. Jesus was hungry, not having eaten for forty days, and he was tired, thirsty, and vulnerable. Those are the times the Devil will attack, so be prepared and recognize where the attack is coming from.

You're physically vulnerable. If you're hungry, sick, ill, unemployed, or struggling in any way, you're physically vulnerable. Think about how you feel when you don't get enough sleep. You're grouchy, short-tempered, and impatient. Those are all things that attract the Devil.

You've recently been attacked. When the Devil attacks you once, he'll circle back around again, hoping to get you when you're weak. Once you've come under attack, you're often left exposed, weak, and vulnerable. Even if you've fought back successfully, you are still in a vulnerable place. That's when the Devil will circle back and attack again. Be prepared. It's not nearly as powerful or devastating when you expect it.

DEVELOPING SEVERAL STREAMS OF ADDING VALUE TO OTHERS

Unless you bypassed the rest of the book and came directly to this chapter, you know I am a very strong advocate of not putting all your eggs (money) into one basket or business. But there's more than just worrying about putting all your financial investments into one business. We should also find several ways to add value to the lives of others. Doing one thing to help others means you will probably be blessed in one area of your life. Increase the ways you help others by volunteering at non-profits, serve in your place of worship, get involved in professional and civic associations, become a mentor, and support local small businesses. People who make it a point to have multiple streams of adding value to others find themselves with multiple streams of income.

HAVING MORE THAN ENOUGH TO MEET YOUR AND YOUR FAMILY'S NEEDS

This comes from watching my own father gamble away a big part of his paycheck each week when I was younger. It wasn't until years later that he realized how this was affecting him and his family. I'm very aware of the fact that it's possible to make enough money to take care of your own family but then not do so. The old saying "charity begins at home" means pay yourself and meet your needs first.

I'm a firm believer in making sure you and your family's financial, spiritual, and physical needs are met and that you have enough to cover any emergency. We can still give and be generous in other ways while tending to our own needs, but unless you are on a solid foundation yourself, you can't help others as much as you otherwise could.

When we have enough or more than enough to meet our own and our family's needs, then we are free to do more.

WEALTH IS LEGACY COMBINED WITH RICHES

There is nothing wrong with having wealth or money. Being rich is not a sin, not evil, and shouldn't be your only goal. It's the *love* of money God worries about. If you're worshipping your bank account, then something's wrong. If you look at Job and many other people in the Bible, God blessed them. They were rich! But they didn't use their wealth to build up pride or to squirrel it away. They used it to create a legacy to help family and show how generous God was. Go and do the same. There's a parable in the Bible that states: "a wise man leaves an inheritance to his children's children." According to the parable, it's not wise to leave nothing for your children when you die. Make sure your children and grandchildren do not have to experience the same struggles you encountered as a child. Get a life insurance policy. It's a selfless act that shows you care about your family's well-being.

Wealth is not a level of riches. Many of us believe that there is a certain amount of money that makes you wealthy, like $50 million or more. Our perception of wealth aligns with our view of false success. Wealth is when your legacy generates income from generation to generation. For example, pass the family business down to your children, leave a rental property to your grandchildren, or write a "how-to" book to help entrepreneurs. Many celebrity millionaires "die broke." Most lasting legacies are built from everyday people.

REDEFINING THE STATUS QUO BELIEF IN WHAT SUCCESS IS AND EXEMPLIFYING WHAT THAT IS

Remember when I talked about drug dealing promoting a false sense of success? You don't have to be a drug dealer to push a false image of success. People do it all the time when they feel pressured to buy a new, expensive car, live in an expensive home, or dress in ways that show off their money. True success is not about how much money or how many things you have. It's not about being seen with celebrities or on television.

True success is being able to help your family, friends, and community by pursuing your passion and fulfilling your purpose. It's about being able to be authentic, honest, and genuine with people. It's about the legacy you're creating and the people you're able to help. It's about being the person God wants you to be. You don't have to follow the status quo. You can define and create your own standard of success and then share it with others. You'll find, as I did, that people are relieved when they realize they don't have to keep up appearances but are loved and respected for who they really are. Take time to sit down and define what success really means to you and why. If you think that you need to be a certain way or type of person to impress others in order to be a success, think again.

BEING WHOLE: PHYSICALLY, MENTALLY, AND SPIRITUALLY

It's hard to be a success when you're sick. And by sick, I mean physically, mentally, or spiritually. Success needs a strong foundation to build on. If you're depressed, get help. If you're physically sick, get help. If your spiritual life is nonexistent, get help. None of us can do life alone. God didn't set us up to be that independent. Relying on others and seeking help, either professionally or personally, is part of God's plan for us. Before you try to be a success in business, make sure you're building on a sound foundation. Lose that weight. Stop smoking. Exercise. Attend church. Work on your own issues. Get healthy. It seems obvious and simple, but you'd be surprised how many of us work hundred-hour weeks and push our bodies too hard, then end up in the hospital or divorce court. There has to be a balance.

RECEIVING ETERNAL LIFE.

You may have read this whole book or just jumped ahead to this section and started reading. You may be saying, "What's all this talk about God?" You may not know anything about Jesus Christ, or you may have been raised in the church or around faith and just ignored it or thought it was stupid or silly. I wasn't always a believer. Many of us don't run into God or Christ until later in life. But once you do, it's really, really important that you sit up and take notice and acknowledge Him.

The Bible not only presents a clear path to eternal life, it explains why we need to act to claim eternal life! We are all born into a life of sin. No one is sinless. We have a sin debt that we owe to God but no way to pay for it. None of our solutions—living a moral life, being religious, or doing more good deeds—can resolve our sin problem.

The good news is, God Himself has provided the solution, one that both satisfies His demand for justice and yet grants us mercy. He sent His Son to pay the sin penalty we owe. Jesus Christ was qualified to be our substitute because He alone, being both God and man, never sinned. He willingly took our place on the cross and experienced the full measure of God's wrath against our sinfulness. In dying for us, Christ secured our salvation by paying the debt for all our past, present, and future sins. When we trust in Jesus and surrender our life to Him, He becomes our personal Savior and Lord. The bad news is: you can't earn salvation. Nothing you or I can do would ever be good enough to satisfy God's demand for justice. The good news is: Christ died *for* us. We don't have to do anything other than acknowledge that, believe it, accept it, and act on it.

FOLLOWING CHRIST FEARLESSLY

Whether you just accepted Christ or accepted Him a long time ago but haven't done much to get to know Him, now's the time. It's only following Christ fearlessly, regardless of what the world and your friends and family say, that catapults you into the realm of success as the God who created you has planned for you. Find a church that preaches the word of God, the saving power of the blood of Christ, and not a "prosperity gospel."

Prosperity gospel, also called the "health and wealth gospel" or the "gospel of success," is a religious belief among some Christians who hold that financial blessing and physical well-being are always the will of <u>God</u> for them, and that faith, positive speech, and donations to religious causes will increase one's material wealth. They tend to see God as a sort of spiritual ATM machine or Santa Claus. They think the Bible is simply a contract between God and humans that says that if humans have faith in God, He will deliver security and prosperity. If you read the Bible, that's not true. All the disciples, except for John, were tortured, whipped, beaten, or crucified, or died horrible deaths for their faith in God! The prosperity churches will place an emphasis on getting stuff from God (wealth, riches, job success, and so on) rather than on learning how to know, love, and trust God and follow His commandments to love one another and worship Him above all else. Oddly enough, the pastors who preach the prosperity gospel believe you must donate lots of money to them to achieve God's prosperity.

According to the Bible, God blesses who He chooses to, both sinners and the saved. He doesn't bless them for their good works, visions, or donations. He blesses those who do His will and love and worship Him. And sometimes those blessings are received here on Earth, and sometimes we won't see them until we're in heaven with Him.

HAPPINESS

Happiness is different things to different people. However, I believe true, lasting happiness is being content with who you are and the plan God has for your life. Happiness is directly connected to fulfilling the passion and purpose for your life. Some people that have riches, fame, and everything else most people thinks should make you happy, are depressed and unhappy. The reason is they have not discovered their why and purpose. Even though they have so much, they feel empty and unfulfilled.

Happiness and true success is one in the same. They both are the result of passion driven occupations, ministries, relationships, and civic activities. The pursuit of riches and fame alone, in most cases, will lead to disappointment. I've made many decisions based on the lure of fame and fortune only to lose money and end up less popular with the people that was depending on my success. The times I was in tune with God's inspiration (when things go your way or people unexpectedly do things for you) I found myself doing things that I love, like making signs, running transportation businesses, and operating an insurance agency.

Be on the lookout for signals that you're on the right path. Answered prayers, doors opening up for you, people going out of their way for you, and unexpected calls and emails are common signs that God's inspiration is pointing you in the right direction. Make your passions, talents, and desires the fuel for your purpose and you will forever experience true success and a level of happiness others can't find.

www.ingramcontent.com/pod-product-compliance
Lightning Source LLC
Chambersburg PA
CBHW071423040426
42445CB00012BA/1268